THE
Emotionally Intelligent
REAL ESTATE AGENT

Hendrie Weisinger, Ph.D.

IT'S A BIRD, IT'S A PLANE

ISBN 978-0-615-58793-6

It's a Bird, It's a Plane
www.drhankw.com

Cover and text design by John reinhardt Book Design

ISBN: 1477568093
ISBN 13: 9781477568095

Library of Congress Control Number: 2012909869
CreateSpace, North Charleston, SC

Printed in the United States of America

PRAISE FOR *BOOKS BY DR. HENDRIE WEISINGER*

From "The Emotionally Intelligent Real Estate Agent"
"For 12 years I have put together events to educate and inspire Real Estate Agents and I have never seen a book or a speaker empower more real estate agents than Dr. Weisinger."

Sweeney Agency

From "Emotional Intelligence at Work"
"Emotional Intelligence at Work is your antidote to job related stress. It is healthy and nutritious for your mind and your body."

Dr. Art Ulene, The Today Show

From "The Power of Positive Criticism"
"At long last, a book that demonstrates how giving and taking criticism increases the bottom line. Practical, practical, practical!!!"

Rita McGlone, Associate Director, Executive Education,
The Wharton School of Business

From "The Anger Workout Book"
"Using this book is a goal for every One Minute Manager – a praising if you do, a reprimand if you don't, a crime if you don't lead others to it!"

Kenneth Blanchard,Ph.D. , Co-Author of
The One Minute Manager

From "The Emotionally Intelligent Financial Advisor"
"Dr. Weisinger's book addresses the major gap in the training of financial agents—applying their emotional intelligence. For those agents who want to learn how to get, keep, and work with clients, this is the book to read."

—DR. RICHARD GEIST, *Harvard Medical School, Author of* Investor Therapy

Acknowledgments

Producing a book is like building a house. It starts with a great foundation. My foundation was provided by Mr. Ken (Kenny) Shapiro, president of Triple Nickel Realty (triplenickelrealty.com). Kenny's knowledge and expertise in all facets of the real estate industry and business provided me with a depth of knowledge and insight that would have been impossible for me to obtain elsewhere. From finding listings, obtaining loans, construction, penetrating markets, selling strategies, and cosmetic repairs, to the ins and outs of hidden costs, he educated me. Most importantly, his friendship provided a most solid foundation, immune to earthquakes, hurricanes, tornadoes, and a volatile economy. This book would not have been written if I had not known him for over forty years.

Next is an example of an emotionally intelligent real estate agent: Ms. Audrey Demetres. She provided me with a model of how best to deal with and master the daily real estate challenges. I will best describe her as the cover girl for the emotionally intelligent real estate agent.

Derek Sweeney knows a good property when he sees one. His encouragement to write this book and get it listed so we could sell it was the catalyst for taking action.

A book, like a house, needs to look good. John Reinhardt has my appreciation for staging the book to look like a great buy. In effect, he took the "house" I gave him and turned it into a "home."

Finally, Mr. Shapiro has also taught me the importance of being expense conscious. My time is worth money, so I am sure that all my other friends who have supported me and are delighted with my success will understand when I "cut my time" to write them an acknowledgment. They know who they are and how much I love them.

Hendrie Weisinger
January 5, 2012

PS: I always have time to acknowledge my wonderful children, Bri, and Danny. Expensive?—they are priceless!

Contents

The Emotionally Intelligent Real Estate Agent

ASK ANY REAL ESTATE AGENT, "What's the most important attribute for selling a house?" and almost all will say, "Location, location, location." They're all wrong! The most important attribute for selling a house, or getting a listing for that matter, is EI, EI, EI—that is short for emotional intelligence, and when you develop and apply yours, you are on your way to becoming a success.

Consider this: When you are an Emotionally Intelligent Real Estate Agent (EIRA), you come to work each day with positive attitudes, ready to increase your bottom line and make a huge difference in the lives of your clients. You find it easier to manage your emotions, enabling you to stay motivated in difficult times, bounce back faster from setbacks, and increase your results-oriented behavior. While others struggle to get listings and attract and keep clients, you enhance and develop your client relationships by communicating your ideas more effectively, responding productively to your client's criticisms, and adeptly retain and handle emotionally aroused clients, especially in times of volatile markets. You leave work feeling energized and productive, with lots of positive anticipation for the next day, irrespective of whether the market is stagnant, dropping, or improving.

This book helps you become an emotionally intelligent real estate agent by teaching you how to develop and apply your emotional intelligence in the daily scenarios that determine your success. Here are a few of those scenarios in which applying your EI spells success, and a lack of it spells disaster.

- It is your agency's caravan day, and your new listing is a charming three-bedroom home, with a spacious kitchen and a family room with great built-ins. This will be the first stop. You've worked hard to get the listing. You're excited, you've studied the comps, and you believe the asking price is on the money. Within minutes of your showing, you're told, *In this market, it's way overpriced, It's not as nice as the house a few streets over, The master bedroom is small,* or *The house needs a lot of work.* All eyes are now upon you, eager to hear your response to the unexpected objections. Your anxiety starts to rise. You feel the telltale signs: Your heart pounds, your breathing speeds up, and your palms start to sweat. You respond to your colleagues defensively, and they leave unimpressed, with no intention to tell their clients about the charming home.

- Your secretary tells you Mr. Jones is on the line. His house has been on the market for close to a year, with no showings or inquiries in the last few weeks. The general consensus is that the market is worsening, and at the current price, there is probably little chance of generating interest. In the past, when you've suggested lowering the price, Mr. Jones became extremely angry, often threatening to get a new agent. As soon as you say hello, his response is, "What's going on with my house? Why aren't you getting any interest? And don't tell me to lower the price!" You feel your best response is to hang up.

- It is your first meeting with Mr. and Mrs. Smith, referred to you by their divorce attorney. After introductions, you find out that Mr. Smith wants to sell their house ASAP, while Mrs. Smith wants to get as much as possible, starting with a listing above market price. It is only a matter of time before their arguing causes you to close your office door. Inevitably, they ask you for your input, and you are well aware that alienating either one will cost you the listing. Your head starts throbbing.

The common denominator in these situations and hundreds of others that I have collected from real estate agents is that you can avoid disastrous outcomes if you apply your emotional intelligence.

In the first example, applying self-awareness, managing your emotions, and practicing the skill of taking criticism would allow you to make this listing charming to your colleagues and their potential buyers.

In the second example, being adept at handling emotionally charged clients especially those who bring anger to the table and dealing with adversity will keep you in business. The third calls for you to apply your EI skills of listening, conflict resolution, and understanding how emotions impact negotiation so that you can keep the couple on a goal-directed house-selling course.

Note that in all of these situations it is not your technical skills mortgage information, comparative values, market trends, or financing strategies that make the difference. These are important, but are of little help when clients are yelling at you, are disappointed in your results, or are at ends with each other. Rather, to achieve success in these situations and hundreds of others that you will experience being a top agent requires you to apply your emotional intelligence..

WHY IT PAYS TO BECOME AN EMOTIONAL INTELLIGENT REAL ESTATE AGENT

Emotional intelligence, specifically, refers to your ability to use your emotions, moods, and feelings and those of others to enhance your results.

For you, emotional intelligence means being able to turn setbacks into comebacks, responding effectively to emotionally aroused clients especially those who are angry and anxious and staying motivated and focused during turbulent times.

It means enhancing your productivity by giving positive criticism to your assistants and team members, taking criticism in a manner that helps you develop, and managing your anger when a client is late or blames you for his house not selling. It also means being able to jazz up those you work with, remain calm when your clients panic, and to work out conflict, whether it is with a client, a fellow agent, or your office manager. In short, emotional intelligence means success.

INCREASING YOUR VALUE

The emotionally intelligent real estate agent understands that emotional intelligence is a valuable property that you own. Like any property you own, it is always a sound, solid, and effective strategy to develop and take care of it so you can leverage it to its maximum value.

Emotional intelligence has five key components, and developing each helps your property become more valuable. Here is a prospectus on each component:

1. High self-awareness. This is the foundation on which all other emotional intelligence competencies and skills are built. High self-awareness is about tuning in to information about yourself. With high self-awareness, you can monitor and observe

yourself in action, so you can influence your actions to make sure that they are working to your benefit. High self-awareness increases your results-oriented behavior.

2. Managing emotions (mood management). Managing your emotions means making your emotional housing system your thoughts, physical arousal of emotion, and behavior work for you. Unlike suppressing your emotions, which deprives you of valuable information that those emotions provide, managing your emotions means understanding them and using that understanding to deal with situations productively. Anger, anxiety, disappointment, and fear do not have to derail you from the track of success or create havoc in your life. Quite the contrary, they can all positively impact your bottom line if you apply your emotional intelligence.

3. Self-motivation. This is the ability to get yourself started, to energize yourself. To be a top real estate agent, you have to be highly focused. You do research, talk with people on the phone, go out to see clients, give presentations, and much more. Where does all this energy come from? How do you energize yourself when the market is bad and a client says, "Take my house off the market, I'm listing with someone else?" Self-motivation is what gives you the tenacity to stay focused and keep to the task at hand. It allows you to stick to the issues, accomplish your mission, and turn setbacks into comebacks. Setbacks are a daily occurrence for most real estate agents, and much of your success depends on how well and how quickly you can bounce back and prevent an emotional downswing from killing your productivity. When you are bombarded with stressful situations and interactions that can leave you in a bad mood, those moods are toxic to productivity, so part of self-motivation is the ability to quickly transform your toxic moods into positive energy.

4. Interpersonal expertise. At work, you do not live in a world of "me." You relate to your manager, your support staff, fellow

agents, and, of course, your clients. Conflicts arise, and you better be able to work them out, lest you see your business decline. You have to know how to take criticism from your manager and give it positively to your support staff if you want their support. Most importantly, you have to win the trust of your clients. To build trust these days, you must respond effectively to the emotional state of your clients. Your interpersonal expertise allows you to handle these daily job tasks.

5. Emotional mentoring. This involves helping other people deal with their emotions, communicate effectively, solve their problems, resolve their conflicts, and become motivated. Emotional mentoring requires that you use your emotional intelligence skills to help your managers and coworkers. In particular, these skills can help you in a slow market when you are dealing with upset clients who demand results.

WHAT'S THE ROI?

Developing your emotional intelligence property will take time and energy, so the return on investment (ROI) should be substantial—and it is. Here are a few of the results you can expect from developing your EI property:

- Quickly gain the trust of clients.
- Stay focused and manage anxiety in turbulent times.
- Deal effectively with emotionally aroused clients.
- Respond positively to clients' criticism in order to increase client trust.
- Turn setbacks into comebacks.
- Enhanced office relationships.
- Stay motivated for the long haul.

- Significantly increase your bottom line.
- Be healthier and happier at work and at home.

The goal of *The Emotionally Intelligent Real Estate Agent* is to help you realize these results by giving you the nuts and bolts for developing and applying your emotional intelligence in the context of your daily activities.

You begin by developing a solid foundation for your EI property the core emotional intelligence capacities so that you can immediately begin to see an increase in value.

Next, you show your emotional intelligence to your staff and client relationships by integrating EI skills into your daily work activities.

Finally, you keep your emotional intelligence on a roll by adhering to the rules that help you maintain your status as an emotionally intelligent real estate agent.

The caravan is about to start..

ONE

Developing Your Emotional Intelligence Property

A T A SEMINAR for real estate agents, I begin by asking, "How well do you manage anger? Can you concentrate when you're anxious? Is it easy for you to bounce back from setbacks? Do you get defensive when an agent criticizes your listing? Do you feel down when you lose a listing? Would you say that you are productive each day?"

Answers vary, but the responses I hear indicate that the overwhelming majority of the several hundred people in the room need to develop their emotional intelligence if they want to be successful. My first message surfaces quickly. Becoming an emotionally intelligent real estate agent (EIRA) begins by investing in yourself specifically by getting your emotional intelligence property to work for you. Becoming aware of your emotions, learning to manage them, and learning how to harness emotions into motivational energy is the plan and result of laying a solid foundation for your EI property.

YOUR EI PROPERTY

High self-awareness, emotional management, and *self-motivation* are the three core features of your EI property. They are your core features because their value depends on nobody else, only you. Developing your core features is how you begin to make your emotional intelligence property pay off.

The first step in developing your EI property is to increase your awareness of your emotions and how they impact your daily results. Self-awareness is the key.

HIGH SELF-AWARENESS: YOUR FIRST CORE FEATURE

High self-awareness is your ability to tune in to your thoughts, feelings, senses, actions, and intentions, so that you can use the wealth of information these factors provide to enhance your results in life. *High self-awareness is your most singular important emotional intelligence asset.* It is the seed that gives birth to all other emotional intelligence competencies and skills. For example, you cannot manage anger if you are not aware that you are angry; you cannot productively respond to anxious clients if you are not aware of their anxiety. You cannot self-motivate if you do not know what direction you want to take.

When you have high self-awareness, you can monitor yourself, observe yourself in action, and influence your actions so that they can work to your benefit. By being aware, for example, that your voice is getting louder and you are becoming increasingly angry at a client, and recognizing that you want to retain this client's listing, you might lower your voice, defuse your anger, and respond to the client respectfully. Raising your self-awareness will give you more compass points to help you successfully navigate your life.

High self-awareness is a skill that anyone can cultivate by following these five steps:

1. Examine how you make appraisals.
2. Tune in to your senses.
3. Get in touch with your feelings.
4. Learn what your intentions are.
5. Pay attention to your actions.

These five steps will help you:

- Develop new ways of observing and processing the experiences that influence your thoughts, so that you can become more aware of those thoughts and see how they are formed.
- Become more tuned in to what your senses tell you, so that you can develop greater awareness of what is going on around you.
- Become more aware of what you are feeling, so you can develop a better understanding of your own emotions.
- Get a clearer picture of the short-term and long-term intentions that influence your actions, so you can stay keenly aware of what you want to accomplish.
- Pay careful attention to your actions, so that they will stay in sync with your intentions and make you more effective in business and in your personal life.

Let's look at how each step helps boost your self-awareness to your advantage.

Examine How You Make Appraisals:
Becoming Aware of How You Think

Appraisals are your interpretations of events that help you define what is happening to or around you. Their roots lie in special qualities and circumstances family background, natural talents, physical appearance, systems of belief that help shape your personality. These combine to form the basis for the unique way you appraise the situations you encounter in daily life. Through your appraisals, you generate the self-statements and expectations that help guide your behavior.

The philosopher Epictetus said two thousand years ago, "Man is not troubled by things themselves, but by their thoughts about them." Psychologists today agree it is the meaning we assign to events that gives them the power to affect us for good or ill.

For example, let's say the mortgage rates spike upward making loans available only to those who have "A-plus" credit. If you make the appraisal, "This is really bad. I am not going to sell any homes," you can be sure your mood will be fear and anxiety. On the other hand, if you appraise the same event as, "Here is a great opportunity to meet really well-qualified buyers," your mood is likely to be enthusiastic.

In other words, it is not the event that causes you to feel good or bad, rather it is how you *appraise* the event that determines your emotional reaction. By becoming more aware of your appraisals your inner dialogues, expectations you can learn how they affect your feelings, actions, and reactions. Armed with this information, you can work to change any self-defeating thought patterns.

Let's say you realize that you tend to see yourself in a negative light. You make this conclusion because you "hear" your self-statements: "This client thinks I'm small potatoes and will not list their house with me." If your lack of confidence causes you to act as if you don't have full command of the market, this kind of self-appraisal can easily become a self-fulfilling prophecy. Once you recognize this tendency, you can start trying to put a more realistic and positive spin on your thoughts: "This client knows the top agents, and he wouldn't be here if he wasn't interested in what I have to say." Such thinking, in turn, can help you relax and behave in a way that exudes greater confidence and competence.

Here are some tips for leveraging your appraisals so that your stock in yourself increases.

- *Listen to how you "talk to yourself."* Pick a regular time of day to talk to yourself, and watch for patterns in your inner dialogue. Stay alert to self-destructive thought patterns, such as:

  All-or-nothing thinking: "If my track record isn't perfect, I'm a total failure." Catastrophic thinking: "If I goof up, it will be a huge disaster for my career." Discounting the positive: "I got the listing, but it was just a fluke." Jumping to conclusions: "I'm sure this client won't like me, even though we've never met."

  Of course, some negative thoughts are perfectly reasonable and appropriate, but many aren't. With practice, you can learn to replace these thoughts with more rational ones, such as, "Nobody is perfect," "One little foul-up isn't going to sink my career," "I got this listing because of my hard work and skill," and "Most of my clients seem to like me, so this one probably will, too."

- *Use "I think" statements.* Have an inner dialogue using assertions that begin with "I think," such as, "I think I'm in over my head here," or "I think this client is out of my league." These kinds of statements help you clarify what you're thinking, thus making it possible for you to examine the truth-value of what you are saying. At the same time, they help you see that you alone determine your perception of events.

- *Seek input from others.* There are several sides to every story, so it always pays to ask others for their take on events. Let's say you're required to attend a daylong workshop on raising self-awareness. You think the whole idea of emotional intelligence is a crock, and you view the workshop as a giant waste of time. But while talking to your office mates at lunch, you realize they see things differently. They think they're gaining valuable information, and they back this up with instances when greater self-awareness might have led to a better outcome. Their examples remind you of similar experiences of your own, and you head into the afternoon with a different mindset. Asking others for their appraisals can help you gauge when your own are dead-on accurate, way off target, or somewhere in between.

- *Focus on the appraisal-reaction link.* Remember that your appraisals not someone else's actions (a client taking his house off the market) or outside events (credit tightens) lead to your emotional and behavioral responses. This gives you power over your own reactions. Suppose a potential buyer takes a phone call in the middle of your showing. You might perceive this as a sign that he's not really paying attention. If you accept this interpretation, you might give up and lose the business. On the other hand, you might see it as a welcome chance to collect your thoughts before the next part of our presentation. The choice and the reaction that results is all yours.

Awareness of your appraisals helps you because it produces accurate, sound, and perceptive thinking, thus increasing the likelihood that you make decisions and choose actions that are in your best interest. It also gives you the ability to modify your appraisals from those that have a discouraging impact on your performance to those that can help you improve it.

Tune In to Your Senses

Your senses seeing, hearing, smelling, tasting, and touching are the sources of all your data about the world. It is through your senses that you pick up information about yourself, other people, and situations you are in. But a funny thing often happens to your senses: the information they gather is filtered and transformed by your appraisals. The higher your self-awareness, the greater your ability to take the filtering process into account and distinguish between *sensory data* and appraisals.

For example, if you see a person frowning, chin down, you could make an appraisal that she feels sad. That could be a misinterpretation.

Maybe she is simply concentrating. To make an accurate appraisal, you need more data. You can get more data through tuning in to your senses, which let you check, clarify, and alter your appraisals when needed.

Imagine your first meeting with a client who has never been a homeowner, let alone a house buyer. You expect him to be relatively unsophisticated, so you launch into a very basic overview of his buying options a kind of "Home and Condo Buying for Dimwits" explanation. You're so sure of your expectations that you don't hear the client say he has considerable experience in real estate development. You don't see him shifting in his seat or notice his eyes wandering during your spiel. And you don't realize until it is too late that you've lost the client's attention by underestimating his savviness.

You could have avoided this mistake by having greater *sensory awareness*, tuning in to the information that your senses provide. By increasing your awareness of the client's sensory data eyes wandering, shifting in his seat you could have made the tentative appraisal that you were losing your client's interest and adjusted your actions to pique him. Your lack of awareness to sensory information derailed you from success.

However, awareness of sensory data is only the first step. You must also make sure that you interpret the data accurately.

Let's say you begin a meeting with a client, and after a few minutes, you notice he is frowning (sensory data). You interpret that he is not very interested in giving you the listing, and as a result you lose some of your enthusiasm. Next, you see him looking at his watch (sensory data) and appraise it to mean that he can't wait for the meeting to be over. Because these appraisals generate self-statements along the lines of "I am wasting my time; I might as well leave," you cut your presentation short and leave without offering your card or a follow-up phone call. You leave feeling dejected, and a negative spell is cast on the rest of your day.

Reality check: Your client frowned because his wife was in the hospital. He looked at his watch to see if it was time to call the doctor. In other words, his reaction had nothing to do with you or your showing; your reactions were based on misappraisals of the sensory data.

Both of these examples illustrate how a lack of, or a misreading of, sensory information can affect your performance and emotional well-being. In the first example, greater awareness to sensory information could have told you that it was time to switch gears. In the second example, a misreading of the sensory data was the culprit for negative feelings.

To make sensory information work for you, you must be able to do two things: first, *increase your perception of sensory data,* and, second, *distinguish between raw sensory information and your analysis of it.* Here are some tips for leveraging sensory information:

- *Take your brain through its paces.* For at least a week, practice sharpening your awareness of sensory data. Let's say you're at your desk first thing in the morning. Pay close attention to the sounds around you, particularly those you usually tune out: a phone ringing in another office, a door closing down the hall, traffic going past your building. Next, focus on the sights, especially those you usually wouldn't bother to register: the book that's out of place, the ding on the edge of your desk, a single brown leaf on your plant. When you go outside, pay attention to the smells in the air. Challenge yourself to see if you can tell what types of food are being served as you walk past a block of restaurants. The idea behind this practice is to become more perceptive to the information that your senses provide. With this additional data, you can conduct yourself more effectively. For instance, instead of being blind to your client's fidgeting in her chair or deaf to her comments, your increased awareness to this data now allows you to adjust your appraisals and speed up your presentation.

- Learn to tell sense from nonsense. You get a lot of information from your senses, but in order to make sense out of the data, you have to interpret it. "You look nervous" is a subjective appraisal of another person's appearance. It is opinion, not fact. In contrast, "I hear a tremor in your voice," "I see a tic over your right eye," or "I feel sweat on your palm when we shake hands" are examples of objective sensory data. Likewise, "I think you're bored" is an appraisal. "I hear your pen tapping on the desk," "I see you staring out the window," and "I feel the vibrations from your foot shaking" are sensory statements.

Making the distinction between sensory data and your interpretations will help you more accurately read the situation and, many times, save you from unwarranted emotional distress. Interpreting the sensory data of a client looking at his watch to mean he has to call the hospital is sure to lead to different feelings than interpreting the same sensory data as boredom.

ON THE STREET

Here's an easy exercise to practice differentiating *sensory data* from your appraisals. Sit down and observe your surroundings through your senses. As you form your perceptions, preface them with the appropriate sensory channel. For example, I *see* people moving quickly, I *hear* people speaking loudly. I *smell* Chinese food. Next, for every sensory statement you make, appraise it three different ways: *I see people talking to each other*: This means people are friendly; this means people are wasting time; this means people have nothing to do. Next, *I hear car horns outside*. This means people are jaywalking; this means there is an accident slowing traffic; this means someone has a flat tire. Do this for each of the sensory statements that you make. Gradually, you will become more and more adept at recognizing and differentiating sensory data from your interpretations. In so doing, you will begin to cut out many inaccurate appraisals of sensory data, thus saving yourself from unwarranted emotional distress and helping you choose your most productive actions.

Get in Touch with Your Feelings
And Their Messages

Your feelings are your spontaneous emotional responses to the interpretations you make and the expectations you have. Like sensory data, they provide important information that helps you understand why you do what you do. They alert you to your comfort level in a situation, and they help you understand your reactions.

Sometimes we're not comfortable with what we feel, and we pretend the feelings aren't there. The problem is that by ignoring or denying emotions, we deny ourselves the ability to work through them. Negative feelings can often fester, leaving us feeling worse than we would by tuning in to them.

Tuning in to our feelings is not something that comes easily to most of us. Part of the problem is that we are often uncomfortable with experiencing certain feelings, especially distressful ones such as anger, sadness, and resentment. If we don't address them, we are prevented from making use of the valuable information these feelings could give us, and from using our emotions intelligently.

What information do your feelings provide? Different emotions communicate different messages. For example:

- *Anger* communicates that something is wrong.
- *Anxiety* communicates uncertainty.
- *Fear* communicates a threat.
- *Depression* communicates feelings of hopelessness and helplessness.
- *Enthusiasm* communicates energy and excitement.

There are many other feelings, of course, but these five are basic aspects of emotional intelligence, and we will focus on them. The point for now is that becoming aware of your feelings allows you to respond to their messages in a way that helps you manage those feelings. For example, a potential buyer's agent has just missed her second appointment this month without calling to cancel. You pretend to yourself that you're not angry, just happy to have an unexpectedly free hour. But when the agent calls the next day to reschedule, you let your irritation show by being curt and sarcastic. You wind up hurting a relationship that needs to be positive.

Let's rewrite this story to give it a happy ending. Instead of denying your anger, let's say you recognize and acknowledge the feeling. This gives you the chance to use your feelings productively. You realize that anger communicates that something is wrong. In your mind, what is wrong is that the agent canceled without calling. You decide that the best thing to do is to speak to her; otherwise the angry feelings will fester. When she calls the next day, you offer to drop by her office. Once there, you calmly bring up the problem of missed appointments and suggest some practical solutions. You wind up agreeing to call her the day before every appointment to confirm, and she'll give you at least twenty-four hours notice if she needs to cancel. The result is likely to be a stronger working relationship grounded in mutual respect.

To get value from your feelings, follow these two tips.

1. *Acknowledge your feelings.* Some feelings are harder to acknowledge than others. It is a lot easier, for example, to acknowledge that we feel happy than sad. Positive feelings are pleasant; negative ones may hurt us. Think about which feelings are easy for you to acknowledge and which ones are difficult to confront. This will make it easier to acknowledge all feelings. Consider the last meeting you had with a client, and recount what you felt.

2. *Do not confuse your feelings with your appraisals.* "I feel it wasn't right that you didn't call me." How can that be? How can we feel "it wasn't right?" Right is not a feeling. It is an evaluative

thought. We frequently express our feelings the way we would thoughts because we don't know exactly how to describe them when we experience them. Feelings expressed like thoughts are known as I-feel-thinking statements rather than as I-feel-emotion statements. A good rule for whether you are making an I-feel-thinking statement is to replace "I feel" with "I think." If the statement makes sense, then it is probably a thinking statement rather than a feeling, or emotional, one. For example, "I *think* it wasn't right that you didn't call me" makes sense. Using I-feel-emotion statements, such as, "I feel angry that you didn't call me," forces you to acknowledge your feelings, and thus become aware of the information they provide.

Following these two tips will help you become more comfortable with your feelings, thus making it easier for you to acknowledge them and use the information they provide.

ON THE STREET

Keep a *feeling journal*. At the end of the day, or at different times of the day, make a note of the feelings you have experienced in the preceding hours. You might even rate them on a scale of 1 (little) to 9 (high) in regard to their intensity. For example, 1 (low anger) to 9 (very angry); 1 (low enthusiasm) to 9 (high enthusiasm). Doing this daily will increase your awareness of how and what you feel each day. After a week, ask yourself the following questions:

- What feelings do I experience the most?
- What feelings do I experience the least?
- What do my feelings tell me about myself and my workday?

Pay attention to the physical sensations you have every day. We touch thousands of things daily, yet it would be hard for you right now to get a good "feel" for each and every thing. For instance, what does your desk feel like? Can you get a good feel for its texture? Can you remember the feel of the fabric of yesterday's clothes? These sensations often escape us, even when we are directly experiencing them. Just because we're touching does not mean we're feeling. Studies show that as physical sensitivity increases, so does psychological sensitivity. Give yourself assignments of touching something smooth, soft, hard, and so on. The exercise will increase your ability to identify your feelings.

Learn What Your Intentions Are

Intentions often reflect your immediate desires what you would like to accomplish today, in a specific situation, or, perhaps, in the coming week. Intentions can also refer to long-term desires what you would like to get done by the end of the year or over the course of your lifetime.

The value in becoming fully aware of your intentions is that you can use the information to help you develop a strategy for your course of action.

Let's say you've been given a ticket to a high-profile charity event this evening. You know this is a golden opportunity to mingle with the rich and famous, but what do you *really* want to accomplish tonight?

A. Make a good impression, so that someone might call you later or recommend you to a friend.
B. Introduce yourself around and maybe even set up a meeting or two later this week, as a result.
C. Have a good time; it is free food, after all.

To make the most of this opportunity you must tailor your actions at the event to your intentions.

- If your answer is A, you might focus on circulating, chatting, and, of course, casually handing out your card when the occasion arises.
- If your answer is B, you might take a more direct approach to introducing yourself, describing what you do, and suggesting a meeting.

- If your answer is C, you might decide to take the night off from thinking about business, because everyone deserves a break now and then.

Learning what your intentions are helps you develop a strategy for action. Awareness of your intentions can also help you rid yourself of counterproductive behavior. For example, you might want to yell at your assistant because she forgot to give you an important message, and you are furious. You also want her to feel comfortable working with you, which she wouldn't if you were to yell at her. If you recognize that your true intention is to have a good working relationship with your assistant, then you are more likely to manage your anger and less likely to yell when she errs.

If you're like most people, it is the short-term intentions that cause you the most headaches. Often, the problem is figuring out what you really desire, as opposed to what you *think* you want or what other people say you should want. As confusing as it can be to sort out your true intentions, it is well worth the effort.

Consider the three intentions for the charity event cited above. While all are perfectly valid, each implies a different course of action to reach the goal. In other words, *the more aware you are of your intentions, the better you can ensure that your actions are in sync with your wishes.*

Of course, you wouldn't consciously try to sabotage your own wish fulfillment. Yet that's exactly what can happen when your intentions and actions operate at cross-purposes, often without you even realizing it. Sometimes, this is because you have a hidden agenda. Perhaps your apparent intention is simply to make more money. However, your secret desire is to win the admiration of colleagues. So, recognizing your true intention doesn't mean abandoning your financial goals, but it does suggest that you might need to spend more time networking with other advisers.

A bigger problem arises when two intentions are in direct conflict. Let's say your goal is to sell more homes, but you also want to pursue personal hobbies during work hours. This second desire might get in the way of spending enough time helping clients get their home ready to be shown, which certainly would make it harder for you to achieve your first desire. In this case, it is important to clarify your true intentions. If your top priority really is to sell more homes, then you need to find ways to stay more focused on professional responsibilities during the workday.

How can you discern your true intentions so you can profit from them? Follow these tips:

- *Identify your intentions at the start of each day.* Make yourself aware of your intentions before work starts by making a list of what you want to accomplish, such as building relationships with clients, finding prospective clients, and reviewing new listings. Keep the list on your desk and, by frequently gazing at it, you will remain aware of your daily intentions. You then can decide what behaviors you must adopt to realize your intentions.

- *Tune in to your behavior.* In general, when you do something, it is because you want to do it, or at least because you stand to gain something by it. As a result, your actions are good clues to your intentions. Let's say you're headed out the door at 5:00 p.m. to meet some friends for dinner when a potential calls and asks if you can drop by his home in an hour. You can hardly believe it when you hear yourself agreeing. What were you thinking? Based on your behavior, probably a new listing is more important than having dinner with your friends. Later that night, you tell your friends that you really wanted to be with them, but the fact is, your behavior shows otherwise it was really more important to get the listing.

- *Use your feelings to surface your intentions.* When you follow your intentions, you feel good because you are doing what you want to do. When you do not act in accordance with your true intentions, you experience psychological distress, as you have put yourself in a setting that you would rather avoid. When you feel bored at a meeting or impatient with a client on the phone, these feelings tell you that you want to escape the situation you want to leave the meeting or end the call. On the other hand, if you feel good, you are probably where you want to be or doing what you want to be doing.

Consider this example: Your friend refers her friend to you. Usually this makes you happy, but this time, you recognize that every meeting with one of your friend's friends leaves you uncomfortable and stressed out. You aren't sure why until you think about these feelings. You realize that her friends take up a lot of your time and rarely end up putting their home on the market. You feel angry and think you're wasting your time. You conclude that you really don't want to meet your friend's friends. With your friend, you do some shuffling, get rid of her as a referral source, and guess what? You end up feeling better. You also have freed up time to do what you want to do find better clients.

Thus, awareness of your intentions increases your productivity, because it tells you what you really want to be doing and helps you guide your behavior to get what you want. At the same time, you become more aware of those situations that you want to avoid.

Pay Attention to Your Actions

How do you act with your staff? How do you act with your clients? What actions cause you to waste time, and what actions help you be productive and get the results you want? The degree to which you can provide the answers to these questions is an indication of how aware you are of your behavior the fifth component of your self-awareness.

In contrast to your appraisals, senses, feelings, and intentions, which are internal processes, your actions are external; they're out there for everyone, including yourself, to see. By tuning in to your behavior, you can deduce important information that will help you become more productive. For example, you can cut your time-wasting habits. You can begin generating behaviors that are more productive to client relationships. You can also start deleting your personal behaviors that others find distracting and annoying, and you can gain a greater awareness of your feelings.

You're probably already aware of the way you generally act (while talking to an employee, for example), but you may be less cognizant of the finer nuances coloring your actions, such as speaking loudly. Other people undoubtedly notice these things, however, and use them to draw conclusions about your attitudes and feelings. If you speak loudly, your assistant might think you are angry and become defensive or angry in return, when in truth you are just excited about the plans you're discussing. By becoming aware of your actions, you can learn to control them and communicate more accurately.

Are you aware of which of your actions turn off prospects and cost you clients? Consider your first meeting with a potential client referred to you by a friend. Neither of you has a lot of time, and the client has lots of questions, many of which you have heard before. In fact, before she can even finish her questions, you give the answers. The meeting ends, and she tells you that maybe she will get back to you. Of course, she never does. A week later, when you mention her to your friend, you hear, "Yes, she told me she met with you, but she felt you weren't listening to her." If you had been more aware of your "interrupting style," you could have let her finish her questions, and perhaps she would have been interested in doing business with you.

Are you aware of what you do during the first two hours of work? If your intention is to find new listings, you better make sure your morning actions are taking you in that direction. By being aware of your behavior, you can begin to identify those behaviors that help you improve your business and focus on doing them, rather than engaging in numerous activities that may be interesting and enjoyable (like reading the paper and schmoozing with fellow agents) but provide little to your bottom line.

Being aware of your behavior also gives you important insight into your emotional landscape. Let's say an agent from another agency frequently invites you to see his listings. You note that you always turn down the invitations, with reasons ranging from "I don't have enough time" to "I have something else scheduled." You begin to think about your "refusal" behavior, and as you do, you become aware that seeing other agents' listings makes you feel anxious because you don't think you have the appropriate expertise to find a buyer or to get similar listings. Armed with this awareness, you begin a series of actions—gathering research, mentally practicing the presentation, anticipating questions, and preparing responses. After a while you feel confident, and when the agent again invites you to a showing, you not only jump at the chance, but also have a buyer who would be perfect!

How do you increase your awareness of your behavior? How do you maximize the value of this information? Use these tips.

- *Practice observing your behavior.* Choose an activity that you perform often, such as walking through a home with a client. Then monitor your behavior on several different occasions to look for patterns. Do you walk too quickly? Point out particulars? Lead them or walk behind them? Once you identify habitual actions, think about what they imply. Leading them, for example, might indicate you are hard selling, while walking behind them might suggest you are interested in how they feel. The goal is to promote actions that work for you while eliminating those that work against you.

- *Observe how your actions affect others.* Select one action, and then perform it in several situations to observe others' reactions. Let's say you choose smiling. Make an effort to smile more often at clients during conferences, at coworkers during meetings, and at people from other offices as you pass in the hall. Do people smile back and make eye contact? Do they strike up conversations or invite you to socialize outside of work? Do clients seem more motivated than on previous occasions? Do they vow to tell their friends about you? By observing your actions through the lens of others' reactions, you can learn to engage in constructive behaviors and eliminate destructive ones.

As you become more aware of your behavior and the information it provides, you will find yourself generating actions that give you positive results.

ON THE STREET

Analyze your day. For one week, play close attention to your work schedule, starting with the minute you walk into your office and ending when you leave work. Be tuned in to how you spend your time. Which actions help you take care of business, and which ones deter you? Is your behavior productive in the morning, or in the afternoon? How come? What behaviors do you avoid? Why? What actions do you need to do more of to enhance your business? The end result will be greater awareness to specific actions that can make you more productive.

Putting It All Together

Naturally, the ultimate goal of high self-awareness is to increase those actions that get you where you really want to be, while decreasing counterproductive thoughts, emotions, and behaviors. To achieve this goal, you must tune in to your own appraisals, senses, feelings, intentions, and actions.

Self-awareness is your core EI asset. Simply put, developing your self-awareness immediately increases the value of your EI portfolio.

The caravan has started!

ON THE STREET

To put all the elements of self-awareness together, try these two exercises:
Review your self-awareness in play. At the end of a workday, write down a brief description of one of your activities. Then look at how each of the five components of self-awareness came into play. Here's an example: An important client calls to explain that your assistant was rude on the phone yesterday. You want to reassure the client of your professionalism and let her know that her business is important to you (intention). Then you notice your voice rising (sense), and realize you are embarrassed by your employee's lapse (feeling). Instead of becoming defensive, YOU tell yourself (via self-statements) that you can't control someone's behavior, but you appraise the incident as an opportunity to show what a good and considerate agent you are. You deliver a gracious apology (action). When you get off the phone, you congratulate yourself on handling the situation so well and on being such a self-aware professional. Thinking about your awareness in play helps reinforce the importance of each self-awareness component by showing you how they affect your everyday outcomes. As you see how these factors influence you on a daily basis, you become much more likely to heighten your ability to use them advantageously.
Examine the high self-awareness question. Several times a day, ask yourself these high self-awareness questions. Your answers will serve the dual purpose of developing your self-awareness and keeping you on the track of success.

- How am I thinking—positively or negatively? Are my thoughts helping me make the day productive? How did I appraise my day when I woke up? Did this appraisal put me in a good mood?
- What am I tuning in to right now? How am I interpreting the data I sense?
- How am I feeling? What is the basis for these feelings?
- What do I want? Am I clear on my immediate goals?

- How am I acting? Are my actions matching my intentions? Am I engaging in productive behaviors?

The more you do these exercises, the more you will develop your self-awareness.

MANAGING YOUR EMOTIONS
YOUR SECOND CORE FEATURE

You know the scene: A real estate agent is enthusiastically presenting her listing to her fellow agents. The response is a barrage of critical comments. The agent tries again, but this time, she is thwarted by booming interruptions. Throwing up her hands, she leaves feeling bitter, angry, and resentful toward her colleagues, whom she believes are an obstacle to her success.

So what does it really mean to manage your emotions? It means understanding your emotions and using that understanding to turn situations to your benefit. It also means making sure that you never let your emotions trigger behavior that is counterproductive to your intentions.

When we hear "get control of your emotions" or "chill out," we often take it to mean "stifle your emotions," and a lot of us try to do that. The problem is that suppressing emotions doesn't solve anything. It certainly doesn't make the emotions go away; it usually lets them fester, and that can cause problems.

Managing your emotions means something quite different from stifling them. It means using your thoughts to make good choices about your behavior. It means having the capacity to soothe and shake off your anxiety, gloom, irritability, and even irrational exuberance. Managing your emotions essentially means that you can maintain your emotional perspective.

What about the angry, frustrated agent in the previous scene? What might be a more emotionally intelligent way for her to deal with her situation? Say she first *becomes aware that she is feeling anger* and uses it as a cue that *something is wrong.* What's wrong is that her fellow agents are being critical of her listing.

Then she tunes in to her own thoughts: "They're jealous! I could strangle them!" This agent now begins to have a constructive inner dialogue, and says to herself, "They are making some good points, but I will not let the situation get out of hand. I know the listing is a good one, but I do need to consider their points." Then she tunes in to the physiological changes —fast breathing, pounding heart —that she is experiencing, and she practices some relaxation techniques. She looks at her anger actions—clenching her jaw, making a fist—and stops doing them. Then she gives herself a time-out by going to get a drink of water. Finally, she resolves to have some follow-up meetings with some of her colleagues to come up with some ways to counter their objections.

This part of your EI property shows you ways to manage your emotions. You will see and learn how taking charge of your thoughts, your visceral responses, and your actions helps you deal with your emotions in ways that can greatly increase your productivity.

Your Emotional Operating System

Three separate components of your emotional system are involved in recognizing and managing emotions:

1. Your thoughts, or cognitive processes
2. Your physiological changes, or arousal actions
3. Your behaviors, or action tendencies

Emotions are produced by an interaction of these three components, in response to external events. Each component influences the others—think angry thoughts and your blood pressure and heartbeat are bound to increase. Take a deep breath to relax, and your angry thoughts are sure to diminish. Find yourself yelling, and you can count on your thoughts being loaded with anger. In other words, the three components operate as a system —each affects the other.

A good way to think of your emotional operating system is as a triangle, with your thoughts at one point, your emotional arousal at the second point, and the way you behave at the third. Managing your emotions requires that you take charge of these three components of your emotional operating system. It is your thoughts, physiological changes, and behavior that drive your emotional responses, not someone's actions, or external events.

In the case of the agents who criticize your listing (external event), it is your thoughts ("They are jealous"), your physiological action (heartbeat increasing), and your actions (clenched fist, sarcastic comments) that cause you to experience anger. When you understand this, you recognize that the power to manage your anger and other emotions rests with you, not with your colleagues, client, or anyone else.

Emotional-Management Tools

Because emotions are so powerful, managing them requires potent techniques. Here are four:

1. Take charge of your thoughts.
2. Use relaxation to decrease your physiological arousal.
3. Take control of and generate effective behavior patterns.
4. Take time out to calm down, and even have a laugh.

These four techniques will help you:

- Recognize that your own thoughts, physiological changes, and behaviors drive your emotional responses, and that you can take charge of them to be sure that your behavior is in harmony with your intentions.
- Diminish anxiety, anger, and fear so that you can respond to clients in considered, emotionally intelligent ways.

- Recognize when behavioral patterns aren't working for you, and find ways to change them, so you can move toward your goals with full effectiveness.
- Learn when to walk away from tense situations and calm down, perhaps with some good laughs, to restore your equilibrium and trigger positive feelings.

In other words, these four emotional-management tools help you leverage your emotions into assets that enhance your bottom line.

Managing Your Emotions by Taking Charge of Your Thoughts

Among the many ways that our thoughts influence how we feel is through the things we say to ourselves. Our internal conversations, private speech, thought-talk, or self-statements are the mechanisms that allow us to bring to life the appraisals we make and the expectations we have. The statements that we make to ourselves precede, accompany, or follow the things we feel.

In emotional situations, self-statements play an important part in defining and shaping your emotions. For example, "I'm going to tell this client to shove it. I'm not going to take this crap anymore," or "Jeez, she's a real pain in the ass. I'm going to fix her good." Such self-statements intensify the negativity and prolong distressful emotions long after the incident is over. The goal in taking charge of your thoughts is to be able to use your self-statements in a way that will enhance your results rather than derail you from the success track. There are two steps to take to reach this goal. First, take charge of your *automatic thoughts,* and minimize your *cognitive distortions*—appraisals that make the situation worse. Then, use your thoughts in the form of *constructive internal dialogues* and *instructional self-statements.*

How your thoughts operate. Thoughts that spontaneously pop out and repeat themselves "I could kill him; he never listens to me!" are what we call *automatic thoughts* because they seem to occur without any prior reasoning or reflection.

Being aware of your automatic thoughts is important because it gives you practice paying attention to the specific self-statements you make when you are emotionally distressed or going into a potentially emotionally taxing situation. This awareness then becomes a cue that you need to talk to yourself differently in a way that helps you manage your emotions, rather than have your emotions hijack you. Being aware of your automatic thoughts will also help you avoid *distorted thinking* appraisals that you make that are misconceptions of reality and make the situation more stressful than warranted. Automatic thoughts have the following characteristics:

- *They are private.* Most people talk to themselves differently from the way they talk to others. When we talk to others, we tend to describe our life events in a rational manner. When we talk to ourselves, we are frequently irrational and use horrifying overgeneralizations, such as, "I'm a failure. Nobody will ever love me."

- *We almost always believe them.* Despite their irrationality, automatic thoughts are unquestioningly accepted. They seem plausible because they are hardly noticed. We don't question them or challenge them, nor do we logically analyze their implications.

- *They are discrete and specific messages.* They give us a direct and distinct message about some event, such as "The client thinks I am a fool."

- *They usually appear in brief form.* Automatic thoughts are frequently abbreviated to one word or a transient visual image. For example, an agent might say, "Zip" to tell herself that she will be left with no clients after a mortgage tightening.

- *They are learned.* Ever since we were born, people have been telling us what to think. Our family, friends, teachers, and even the media condition us to appraise events in specific ways.

- *They tend to be catastrophic.* Automatic thoughts tend to act as cues for other thoughts. One depressing thought might trigger a whole chain of depressing thoughts.
- *They are hard to turn off.* Because automatic thoughts go unnoticed, they seem to come and go as they wish.

Here is an example of an automatic thought that typically happens when a client is expressing anger or disappointment about your performance: The automatic thought, "That's it!" really means, "I am finished. He is pulling his listing. My other clients will do the same. I will not have a job. I will have no money. Everyone will leave me. What's the point of living?"

Distorted thinking. Automatic thoughts often lead to *distorted thinking.* This occurs when we make appraisals that are not tuned in to the reality of the situation. You might be five minutes late to an important meeting, but that is a far cry from telling yourself, "This client will think I am totally irresponsible." *Cognitive distortions* tend to make the situation much more emotionally intense than the situation warrants, and thus interfere with making intelligent decisions. This even applies to enthusiastic automatic thinking, because many a less-than-great financial decision can be tied to out-of-control enthusiasm.
Watch out for these common cognitive distortions:

- *Overgeneralizing.* This involves viewing a specific event as evidence of a general rule, when it is actually not. Yes, you forgot your notes for a crucial meeting this morning, but that doesn't mean that you *always* screw up. Such overgeneralizations sabotage your self-esteem. To spot such thoughts, be aware of using the words *always* or *never.* Ask yourself whether you might substitute a less global term: "I *occasionally* forget something, but *usually* I'm quite reliable."
- *Destructive labeling.* This is similar to overgeneralizing, but involves applying an overly broad label to someone else. Let's

say your receptionist neglects to tell you about a call. Okay, she made a mistake, but that doesn't mean she's an idiot. Such labeling creates the false impression that the situation is irrevocably bad —that there's nothing you can do to make it better. On the other hand, if you focus only on the missed call, you can look for ways to prevent the error from happening again.

- *Mind reading.* Many of us assume that we know what another person is thinking, feeling, or intending, when we actually don't. If a client cancels two appointments in a row, for example, don't necessarily assume that he's planning to jump ship. Perhaps he's just tied up at work or has a family member in the hospital. You never know what's actually going on until you ask. You might say, "I noticed that you missed your last two appointments, and I'm concerned. Are you still interested in buying?"

- *Should and ought.* This involves having rules for how you expect others to act, which just sets you up for disappointment and anger when they don't behave the way you want them to. Let's say you think a good real estate agent should put work before play. You're disillusioned to hear your mentor say that she takes off early three afternoons a week to go to the gym. Your inflexible attitude keeps you from seeing her point of view and possibly learning something. Maybe the energy boost she gets from working out and the contacts she makes at the gym more than compensate for the time away from the office. Keeping an open mind about other people's behavior pays off.

- *Magnification.* Blowing the small stuff out of proportion is common. Suppose you sent a mass e-mail to several clients before realizing your PC had a virus. If you tell yourself that the situation is a disaster —all your clients will hate you, and your career will be over —you may be too overwhelmed to act productively. However, if you manage to hang on to your emotional perspective, you can see that this is a bad situation, but one that can be fixed. At worst you'll have to spend the afternoon calling the recipients to warn them not to open your e-mail. When you catch yourself thinking in terms such as *disaster* and *catastrophe,* be aware that you may be exaggerating the importance of an event.

Learning to avoid distorted thinking is critical. These tips are worth taking:

- *Don't overgeneralize.* Your boss isn't listening to you today, but it isn't true that he never listens to you.
- *Avoid destructive labeling.* She's being a bit of a jerk today, but she's not always a jerk, and you know it.
- *Avoid mind reading.* Don't guess what another person's motives, thoughts, and feelings are. If you really want to know, consider saying, "You seem dissatisfied with my performance. Are you?"
- *Don't have rules about how others should act.* Recognize that people are different and have their own sets of rules. Don't set yourself up for disappointment and anger when they don't behave as you want them to. Stay away from such words as *ought, should,* and *must.*
- *Don't inflate the significance of an event.* Everyone is entitled to a mistake now and then; don't let the small stuff trigger negative automatic thinking about other people or yourself.

ON THE STREET

For the rest of today, and tomorrow, try to catch yourself having automatic thoughts. You will learn a lot about how you talk to yourself, and that's an important thing to know. Don't write anything down; just pay attention. Listen to what you are thinking, and you will gain some insight into your automatic thoughts. Notice whether you overgeneralize, engage in destructive labeling, indulge in mind reading, have rules about how others should act, or inflate the significance of events.

After you have spent some time "hearing" your thoughts, look at the following pairs of sentences. From each, select the one that better describes what you "heard" when you paid attention to your automatic thinking.

- I heard myself overgeneralizing about a colleague or friend. I didn't overgeneralize.
- I heard myself giving someone a destructive label because I was angry. I didn't give anyone a destructive label.
- I caught myself having rules about how others should act. I didn't have rules about how others should act.
- I caught myself inflating the significance of an event. I didn't inflate the significance of any event.
- I heard myself having automatic thoughts triggered by enthusiasm. I didn't have automatic thoughts triggered by enthusiasm.

Repeating this for a few days will help you rid yourself of distorted thinking and the problems it creates.

Constructive internal dialogues and instructional self-statements. Combating distorted automatic thinking and replacing it with constructive inner dialogue is a great way to take charge of your thoughts. You can do this by a method I call *Checking Things Out*.

I've asked many real estate agents, "What makes you angry?" A popular response is, "When you have a good idea and your boss won't listen." A lively discussion follows focusing on their emotional responses in such a situation. I sum it up this way: "The boss doesn't accept your marketing idea and tells you to go away. Your automatic thoughts are, 'He's an idiot. He never listens to me. He hates my ideas. He doesn't respect me.' You feel belittled, maybe even dejected. You leave angry. The rest of your day is bad."

Everyone agrees that this is an accurate description of the scene, and everyone also agrees that if the incident occurs in the morning, the rest of the day is spoiled.

I tell them, "Over the years, I have developed a four-step process that can help you in situations that typically create emotional distress, preventing you from doing your best. The basic strategy is to get rid of your distorted, automatic thoughts such situations typically provoke, and then help yourself by having a constructive internal dialogue. I will show you how it works using the same example:

"He's an idiot. He never listens to me. He hates my ideas. He doesn't respect me."

First, acknowledge the emotion: "I'm really angry at George!" Then knock out distorted statements by challenging their truth-value and rephrasing them to the specific situation.

- "George is an idiot" (destructive labeling) becomes "George is no idiot. I'm just angry that he's not doing what I want."
- "He never listens to me!" (overgeneralization) becomes "Is this really true? Just the other week, he spent a good half hour listening to my concerns about a new listing."
- "He doesn't respect my ideas" (mind reading) becomes "In the past, he's been supportive of many of my ideas. I wonder why he isn't sold on this one. I need to find out. Maybe I'm missing something, or maybe more dialogue will make it a better idea, one he will support."

After some more discussion, I summarize the useful procedure: "Checking things out is a four-step process for avoiding automatic thinking and developing constructive inner dialogue." The four steps are:

1. Acknowledge the emotion.
2. Check your thoughts for the distorted thinking styles and self-statements that evoke the emotion.
3. Restate the distorted statements so that they are reality-based.
4. Reinterpret the event free of cognitive distortion.

To make sure the process is clear, I do it as a soliloquy:

George is such an idiot. He makes me so angry. I feel as though he never listens to me or to any new ideas from anyone, and he doesn't respect me. Wait a second, get a hold. Is what I'm telling myself really true? Well, not exactly. Okay, he gave me credit for a new idea last week in front of everyone —and thanked me. So it's this one he thinks is harebrained, not all my ideas. Is that a guy who doesn't respect me? But he called this one a harebrained idea! He always...nah, last week he respected me. It's just this one idea he thinks is harebrained. I wonder why. I never asked him. Maybe I'd better go talk with him.

Bottom line is, I'm angry...better yet, frustrated, that I cannot get George to go for this idea. But he is a smart guy, and I will talk to him again about it, and maybe we can come up with something he will support.

And yes, there is applause!

Instructional self-statements. A second and powerful way to get away from the automatic thoughts that can work against you is arming yourself with *instructional self-statements* that help guide you through emotionally stressful situations. They are particularly useful when you know you are entering a situation that can be emotionally charged or a situation in which you must be at your emotional best. Instructional self-statements will reassure you and suggest the course you should follow.

ON THE STREET

1. Identify an upcoming situation, such as a presentation or a difficult client meeting that might trigger negative automatic thoughts for you. Imagine the emotions that might be involved, such as anxiety or anger. Write them on an index card.

2. Next, think of three instructional self-statements that would cut off your negative automatic thoughts in that situation and help you manage your emotions, and write the statements on the index card.

Read the sample self-statements above for inspiration and ideas. Use any instructional self-statements that apply to your situation and/or create your own. Remember to make them very specific. Instead of "'relax," make it "breathe slower."

3. Keep the index card in sight so that it will be a constant reminder of how to talk to yourself when you encounter the situation.

4. Create a card for as many emotionally arousing situations you can think of. Doing so will help you replace your old, automatic, counterproductive thoughts with productive self-statements. Inevitably, it will become second nature to use them. When this happens, your productivity will soar!

In these tough situations, your automatic thoughts might not match your intentions. Instructional self-statements will help you stay focused, so you can achieve what you intend to achieve and avoid derailing yourself. Here's how to use instructional self-statements:

1. Cut off negative automatic thoughts that don't match your intentions.

2. Replace the negative automatic thoughts with instructional self-statements —constructive thoughts —that will help you behave in a way that is beneficial to you.

Here are some examples of instructional self-statements:

•   "I don't need to get defensive."
•   "The branch manager knows I had no control over the termite inspection report"
•   "I will pay attention to the positive things the client says, not just the negative ones."
•   "I am fully prepared for this meeting."
•   "I know that my planning is sound."
•   "I am sure that my idea is good."
•   "I will acknowledge and handle the client's concerns."
•   "I will ask a question when something is unclear."

- "I will ask how we might resolve the situation together."

Here's a reliable tip: Use *emotional distress* as a signal that it is time to use your instructional self-statements and to have a constructive internal dialogue that challenges the validity of your automatic thoughts. Doing so will immediately allow you to begin the process of managing your emotions.

Managing Emotions by Regulating Your Physiological Arousal

All jokes aside, cavemen and real estate agents do share some traits.

Imagine that you're living in the Stone Age and that you're out hunting for a nice juicy mastodon for dinner. Suddenly, you come across a saber-toothed tiger, and you immediately turn tail and flee. Later that day, you run into a member of a rival clan that is challenging your clan for territory. This time, you stand your ground and fight. Your outward reaction is different, but in both cases, your inward responses are the same—as your body swings into high gear, you experience an increase in your heart rate, blood pressure, breathing rate, muscle tension, and perspiration.

Now imagine that you're a twenty-first century real estate agent. The market is slow, calls from worried clients are up, and a new kid on the block is taking listings for cut-rate fees. As tempting as it might seem, you know you shouldn't run away from the phone or punch out your competitor. But when one of your clients mentions they want to pull their listing or want you to cut your percentage, your body automatically reacts to the perceived threat with the pre-programmed fight-or-flight response. Your heart pounds, your breathing speeds up, your jaw clenches, and you even start to sweat.

These kinds of physiological changes serve as important indicators that your emotional perspective is changing. In other words, they're signs that you have moved from a calm state to one of heightened arousal. By noticing these signs, you are taking an important step toward calming yourself. This, in turn, helps you think clearly and behave in a way that helps you match your behavior to your intentions.

Think of yourself as the thermostat for your own physiological arousal. First, you need to register any changes that occur, much as a thermometer registers a change in room temperature. You do this by becoming more aware of your own heartbeat, breathing, and perspiration. Then you control those changes, just as a thermostat can be used to adjust the heat.

The most effective way to control your physiological changes is to increase your awareness to when you are experiencing stress. By doing so, you reverse the physiological changes that occur with arousal. Your heart rate, blood pressure, breathing rate, and muscle tension decreases, and perspiration returns to normal. At the same time, you slow down your emotional arousal. This gives you a chance to think things through and make productive choices about how to behave, whether it is beginning an important showing, or responding to critical agents.

Arousal indicators. Feelings tend to be associated with specific physical sensations —nervousness with a jittery stomach, anger with warm cheeks, for example. We refer to the physiological changes behind the sensations as *arousal indicators*. Before you can learn to relax in the heat of the moment, you must first be able to recognize your arousal indicators, for these are the cues that tell you it is time to relax. The faster you recognize your arousal indicators changing, the faster you can begin to manage your emotions.

ON THE STREET

For a day or two, pay close attention to changes in your physiological arousal level, especially your heart rate, breathing rate, and perspiration level. Get to know how your own arousal responses work, how you experience arousal, and what sets off your responses. Some helpful questions to accomplish the task include:

- In what situations do you feel most aroused?
- What do your arousal indicators feel like when you are tired?
- What do they feel like when you are stressed?
- What do they feel like when you are happy?
- What do they feel like when you are anxious?
- What do they feel like when you are dejected?
- What do they feel like when you are angry?

Compare your arousal indicators across different situations. The more you do this, the easier it will become to recognize when you need to relax and clarify your thoughts and intentions.

Developing your relaxation response. Your *relaxation response* (RR) is a protective mechanism to counter the harmful physical and mental effects of emotional distress. Specifically, learning to use your RR helps you short-circuit emotional arousal before it becomes too intense, and allows you to appraise the situation accurately —something you cannot do during intense emotional arousal. The ability to think clearly when you are emotionally aroused allows you to handle the situation productively.

Let's say you are doing paperwork and a client calls whose home you've had as a listing for almost a year. She says, "I've been talking with another agent." You feel your heart beating faster as she continues with, "I'm considering making a change." You feel your breath coming more quickly, and you might even begin perspiring. Your arousal level has gone from a calm state to a heightened one.

The best way to manage emotional arousal and support your intention to keep the listing is to diminish the arousal as soon as you become aware of it. If you can instantly note the physiological changes, you have a cue that it is time to calm yourself and thus diminish exaggerated anxiety and fear. Then instead of responding impulsively, you can respond to the client in a considered, emotionally intelligent manner. That response could make the difference between keeping and losing the client.

There are numerous techniques that you can use to develop your RR, such as Transcendental Meditation, Zen, yoga, progressive relaxation, self-hypnosis, autogenic training, and biofeedback. There are, however, four essential components that, irrespective of method, are thought to be necessary to develop your RR.

1. *A quiet environment.* When developing your RR, choose a quiet, calm environment without distractions. This will make it easier to avoid interfering stimuli while you focus on your RR images or statements.

2. *A mental device.* Having a mental device —a sound, word, image, statement, fixed gaze —helps you shift your mind from being externally oriented to being internally oriented. This is important because it enables you to focus on what is happening in your body. The word or image *breaks* your distracting thoughts. It is very important to remember to use the same image, word, sound, or other mental device each time you practice your RR. This consistency will strengthen the association between your thoughts and the desired level of physiological arousal, inevitably leading you to the point where using your mental device automatically elicits feelings of relaxation—Pavlov's dogs, if you like.

3. *A passive attitude.* Passivity is probably the most important component in developing your RR. Distracting thoughts will occur. Don't worry when this happens; just return to your mental device. If you worry about how well you are doing, you may prevent the RR from occurring. Embrace a "let it happen" attitude. Distracting thoughts do not mean that you're doing something incorrectly. Expect them.

4. *A comfortable position.* When you practice your RR, it is important to be in a comfortable position so there is no undue muscular tension. If a position gets uncomfortable, it is a signal that tension is increasing. Switch to a position that makes you feel more comfortable.

The following relaxation exercise is brief, and it covers all the essentials for developing your RR. It takes approximately fifteen minutes. Read it a few times so you can do it on your own. You will first exaggerate muscle tensions before relaxing them. Complete the following steps one at a time:

1. Clench your fist...tighter, tighter...relax.
2. Suck in your stomach; try to make it touch your back...hold it... relax.
3. Clench your teeth; lock your jaw...firmer...firmer...relax.
4. Close your eyelids tightly. Force them together more and more... release.
5. Push your head and neck into our shoulders...release.
6. Inhale...hold it as long as you can...release.
7. Stretch out your arms and legs...stiffer...stiffer...release.
8. Now do all seven steps together. Release, and let a warm, soft, wave flow over your body, relaxing each part in turn as it slowly moves from your head down, around, over, and into every muscle. Especially let it loosen the tension around your eyes, forehead, mouth, neck, and back. Tension out, relaxation in. Let the wave of gentle relaxation dissolve all muscle tension. As you enjoy the feeling, visualize your favorite setting, or say a phrase like, "calm down." Use the same image or phrase every time you practice the exercise.

People differ in how long it takes them to develop their RR, but if you practice ten to fifteen minutes a day, you will feel the benefit of your investment.

ON THE STREET

Once you've conditioned yourself to relax at will, you can use your relaxation response to counteract any change in arousal. Here's how:

1. Imagine a distressing situation, For example, you might think about making a cold call, dealing with a disgruntled client, or talking to your branch manager about a problem in your office. In your mind, go through the steps you would take, and try to make them seem as real as possible by using all of your senses. In the case of a cold call, you might imagine feeling the paper as you run your finger down a long list of phone numbers, looking at a specific number, lifting the phone receiver, hearing the dial tone, and then hearing the tones as you punch in the number. After that, you might imagine hearing someone's voice answering, then hearing your own voice introducing yourself and asking to speak with the prospect. Does this situation typically fill you with anxiety? Then focus on the arousal indicators you might notice as well, such as a racing heart, fast breathing, sweaty palms, or a shaky voice.

2. Introduce your mental construct into the imaginary scene. As you run through each of the steps in your scenario and the arousal indicators that ensue, imagine using the construct to keep your arousal under control. Let's say your voice starts to quiver as soon as you begin introducing yourself. You might silently say, "peace, peace, peace" a few times until you're feeling calmer. Repeat this whole process once a day, for several days, always using the same situation and emotion. When you can shift almost instantly from the first signs of arousal to your relaxation construct, then you know you've learned to associate the construct with the scenario.

3. Introduce your mental construct into a real-life situation. Make an actual cold call, and focus on your chosen thought or images at the first hint of heightened arousal. The ultimate goal is to have your construct kick in just before your arousal shoots up. If you encounter difficulty, go back to practicing the imaginary scenario until you can use the technique effectively in real life.

Managing Emotions by Generating Effective Responses

There are many times when taking charge of your thoughts and being able to relax will help you manage your emotions. There are also times when these tools will be necessary, but not enough to alleviate the emotional distress of the situation —distress that is keeping you from doing your best. For example, the anxiety you feel about a client not responding to your call can be managed by focusing on other tasks or by keeping your thoughts positive, but these are only temporary solutions, as the anxiety will inevitably get to you. Your instructional self-statements may help when a client is yelling at you, but they are of little help in managing the anger that festers long after the incident has passed. You might tell yourself that it is hard to get listings right now, and that will change, but the motivational self-statements will lose their power when the results aren't increased, but your dejection is.

In such situations, the key to managing your emotions is to be able to generate an effective behavioral response —one that helps deal with the emotional distress by a *change in your actions.*

If you've been practicing what you have been reading, you are probably becoming more self-aware. No doubt, developing your self-awareness, especially to your arousal indicators, is helping you recognize when your emotions are derailing you from success. Also, taking charge of your thoughts in the form of instructional self-statements is probably helping you handle yourself professionally. These are important emotional intelligence skills and are necessary, but not sufficient to deal with the above-mentioned examples. To generate an effective behavioral response, you also have to *understand the message of the emotion,* because it is the emotion's message that creates the emotional distress.

Recall that all emotions communicate different messages.

- Anger communicates that something is wrong.
- Anxiety communicates uncertainty.
- Fear communicates a threat.

- Depression communicates feelings of hopelessness and helplessness.
- Enthusiasm communicates energy and excitement.

To generate an effective behavioral response, you must *act in a way that responds to the message of the emotion*. When you do this, you are using your emotions to make intelligent choices. You are applying your emotional intelligence.

ON THE STREET

Identify a situation that creates emotional distress.

- What emotion do you experience —anger, anxiety, dejection, fear?
- What Is the emotion communicating to you?
- What is the best way to respond to the emotion's message?

After a while, it will become second nature to respond to the messages of your emotions. When this occurs you will be applying your emotional intelligence, and you will find yourself becoming much more productive.

For example, take the agent who experiences anxiety because he hasn't heard back from a potential client with a multimillion-dollar listing. He can choose how to respond. If he is overwhelmed by the anxiety, he will probably sit at his desk and do nothing but worry, which actually increases his anxiety of the situation. He could also try to distract himself by putting energy into other tasks. This could be productive, but in all probability, the anxiety will still seep through. Or, he could use his emotions intelligently by recognizing that anxiety communicates uncertainty. What is he uncertain about? In this case, the uncertainty relates to whether the client is going to give him the listing. To act with emotional intelligence, the agent must generate a response that reduces the uncertainty. So, the agent might decide to call the client and ask for some thoughts. Either way, the agent clarifies the client's interest. If the client isn't interested, the agent can move on. If there is interest, it can be pursued. Either way, the adviser can move forward and release the anxiety.

What about the agent who is angry with her branch manager? Instead of developing an ulcer or reliving the incident in living color, or avoiding her manager, or blowing up, she is much better off responding to the message the anger communicates: Something is wrong! There is an injustice. The agent can ask, "What is wrong?" Assuming there are no cognitive distortions, what is wrong is that the agent believes she is not being treated fairly by her branch manager. To act with emotional intelligence, she should devise a plan for opening up a dialogue with her boss to express that she believes she is being treated unfairly. When this is implemented and accomplished, the agent will find that her anger has dissipated, as her response has corrected the wrongfulness of the situation. Her response —the choice to have a discussion about what is provoking her anger —allows her to move on.

What about our dejected agent? Sitting around in mourning is sure to keep her on a downward spiral. But if she remembers that dejection communicates hopelessness, she can then ask herself, "What am I feeling hopeless about?" Her next step is to generate a behavior that will put her in the process of finding new clients. Doing so creates feelings of empowerment, and she can move on rather than ruminate about how bleak the future is.

In all of these situations, acting with emotional intelligence helps the agent alleviate the emotional distress of the situation and move on to perform at his or her best.

To generate effective behavioral responses, you must:

- Recognize the emotion and manage its arousal indicators.
- Understand what the emotion is communicating and act in a way that responds to the message of the emotion.

Managing Your Emotions by Taking Time Out and Having a Laugh

Many of the aforementioned emotional management techniques require an investment of time and energy. In the meantime, to keep you covered on a daily basis, use these crash-proof tips to avoid getting emotionally derailed from the track of success.

- *Take time out.* In a volatile situation, get a drink of water, go to the bathroom, or go for a walk outside or around your floor. However you do it, get away from the situation, so you can calm yourself.
- *Take deep breaths.* Deep breathing slows you down, and you can use it as a method to gain control.
- *Redirect your emotional energy.* Clean up your desk, sharpen pencils, wash your socks, or play oldies on the radio. Do any simple activities that will distract you from your anxiety or anger and at the same time help you get something done.
- *Have a laugh.* We all know that laughter is life's best painkiller. A moment of respite can be quite useful for giving you pause to reappraise things and to get in control of yourself and your situation.

ON THE STREET

Identify an emotionally charged or distressing situation that you are likely to encounter. Prepare an effective emotional operating system sheet. Keep it on your desk as a reminder of how you want your emotional operating system to function when you encounter the situation. If you do this, it will become second nature to keep your emotional operating system tuned for high performance.

Once you manage your emotions, you can begin to develop your third EI portfolio asset—self-motivation.

Putting It All Together

Here's a good activity that will enhance your capacity to use your emotional operating system advantageously.

Write down a description of a recent emotionally charged situation that you did not handle well, one in which you regretted the outcome. Provide the following information:

- What were you feeling?
- What do you suppose you were thinking?
- On a scale of 1 (low) to 9 (high), how strong was your physiological reaction?
- How did you act?

Look at your responses. Did they help you manage the situation productively? *Note the relationship between your thoughts, arousal, and actions.*

Now imagine yourself encountering the same situation. What would you do differently to ensure better results? To help you answer, provide the following information:

- What is the message of the feeling you are experiencing?
- What do you want to say to yourself?
- How will you keep your arousal in check?
- What is the best way to respond?

Now compare your responses, and you will see why and how the desired emotional operating system is more effective, and how the components of the system work to help you get better results.

SELF MOTIVATION: YOUR THIRD CORE FEATURE

Think of an agent whose career has stalled —maybe even your own. Chances are, he or she is suffering from a serious motivational deficiency. Such people tend to fall prey to wasted time, unfocused work habits, and lackluster performance. Their lack of enthusiasm is contagious, and they don't inspire much confidence in others.

Now think of the most successful real estate agent you know. Chances are he or she is a high-energy person. Such people have the drive to make calls, meet clients, do research, and give presentations. They also have the tenacity to stick to a project and see it through. Other folks naturally are drawn to their go-go attitude. Colleagues find them inspiring, and clients trust that they'll get the job done. Self-motivation pays off.

Technically, being self-motivated means you can use your emotions to propel yourself into action for a desired purpose. This is not an easy task, as even the most successful advisers at times feel unmotivated to take on the next challenge.

To leverage your ability to self-motivate, you must be able to turn the four sources of motivation into motivational forces; then you can take care of business and overcome adversity at its worst.

Your Sources of Motivation

1. Your emotional operating system—your own thoughts, actions, and physiological arousal.
2. Supportive friends, family, and colleagues may offer a much-needed push at times.
3. An emotional mentor can help jump-start your enthusiasm. A mentor can be an ordinary person you know and admire, or an inspirational hero, dead, alive, or even fictitious.
4. You can also use your surroundings to help you power up.

Motivating Your Emotional Operating System

You've learned how to use your thoughts, arousal indicators, and behavior to help you manage your emotions. Here are some ways to use those same three components to get you to "Do it!"

Motivational self-statements. Different individuals are motivated by different things. However, there are five key traits that all highly self-motivated individuals share.

1. Confidence
2. Optimism
3. Tenacity
4. Enthusiasm
5. Resiliency

These are the qualities you need to believe so you can do a job, hope for a good result, stay on task until you achieve it, enjoy the process of accomplishing it, and bounce back if things don't turn out quite as well as expected.

One of the best ways to nurture these traits is by motivational self-speaking. Whenever you notice yourself having irrationally negative thoughts —"I'll never get this report done" —you can learn to replace them with more realistically motivational self-statements —"I can write this report. I know the material backward and forward. No one understands it better than I do. I'll finish the report today, and I'll do a good job."

At first, you may feel a bit awkward playing the role of cheerleader to yourself. With a little practice, though, it will start to come more naturally.

Meaningful goals. Continuously setting meaningful goals is another way to keep your motivation high. A meaningful goal is a specific objective that fires up your desire. This arousal can then be transformed into the energy you need to achieve your objective. The trick is to pick a goal that's attainable, yet challenging. Aim too low and you may get bored. Aim too high and you run the risk of getting discouraged and giving up.

When you have a big meaningful goal —doubling your business within three years, for example, *break it down into smaller chunks.* This lets you acknowledge the progress you've made enroute to your final destination. Then set sub- goals, such as increasing business by 10 percent over the same quarter last year. When you reach this milestone, you'll see that you are indeed progressing toward your ultimate objective, and this positive movement can spur you to keep pushing ahead. You become more confident and optimistic.

If you're a glass-half-empty type, you might be tempted to focus only on how far you have left to go. Instead, try to shift perspectives by concentrating on *how far you've come*. Even if you're only a quarter of the way toward your final goal, tell yourself you're 25 percent there. Don't worry about being 75 percent away from your objective, as that will most likely create thoughts that are de-motivating.

ON THE STREET

Give yourself a motivational self-assessment each morning as you first sit down to your desk. For example, "I'm going to have a productive day." Then each time you begin a new task, give yourself another mini pep talk: "I'm going to finish my calls this morning. I'm good on the phone. I can do this well. I'm going to stick with it until I make it through the prospect list." You can even write your most powerful statements on index cards and post them by your desk. "I've got what it takes to be a great financial adviser. Nothing can stop me when I try."

Also, remember that the key is to set goals that are meaningful to you.

Visualize to energize. You can rev up your engine with *mental arousal*. With a little practice, you can learn to intentionally use your thoughts to mobilize your motivation. It is the old "power of positive thinking" philosophy updated for your workplace. To see how easy and effective this can be, try this simple visualization exercise:

1. Close your eyes. Take a few long, deep breaths to relax.
2. Imagine yourself performing the task that you're unmotivated to do. Let's say it is calling a list of potential clients you haven't

heard from lately. Focus on the sensations you would actually feel in this situation—the sight of the list, the smell of a cup of coffee sitting on your desk, the feel of the phone receiver you lift in one hand, the sound of the dial tone, the movement of your other hand as you press the keys, and so on.

3. Imagine yourself struggling with the task and becoming frustrated. Say you call one number after another. The first number is disconnected, you don't get an answer at the second, and you get the runaround from a secretary at the third. Maybe you begin to tap your foot impatiently or slouch dejectedly in your chair.

4. Then, imagine yourself regaining your composure. You sit up straight, but comfortably, in your chair, and you feel calm and in control. See yourself picking up your phone receiver and dialing the next number, with cool efficiency.

5. Next, imagine yourself successfully completing the task. See yourself working your way down the list in a swift and systematic manner. You stay calm when you don't reach a client, and you're pleasantly professional when you do.

6. Finally, imagine yourself feeling good about your success. You've remained focused and made all the calls in record time. You're happy to have this chore out of the way, and you're glad to have touched base with some valued clients.

You'll notice that this mental rehearsal carries over into real-life performance. The explanation is simple: This exercise helps you see a seemingly insurmountable task as manageable after all. By visualizing yourself through it, step by step, you increase your confidence that you are up to the challenge. This, in turn, may spur you to tackle the task in reality.

Playing mind games to win. Another way to kick your career into high gear is with *mind games*. Such games are based on the premise that mental fantasies can guide you to a more upbeat train of thought, which not only helps keep pessimism at bay, but also the arousal generated becomes fuel for enthusiasm. Here's how to play a mental game called "*Day One*".

Let's say you've been asked to make a presentation about retirement planning. You've given dozens of similar presentations before. You know it needs to be done, but you see it more as a chore than a turn-on, so you have trouble getting fired up for this one. Imagine that you're a brand new agent instead, and this will be your debut presentation —your first day on the job.

Approach the chore as you would if this really were your first day. Take a minute to remember how you felt. You probably were filled with enthusiasm and eagerness to get started. By putting yourself in a new frame of mind, you can see the task ahead as a fresh challenge, rather than a familiar drudgery. This, in turn, will help you view it with renewed enthusiasm.

Motivation in motion. A particularly successful real estate agent told me that before every one of his presentations, he goes in his office, does five minutes of the Ali shuffle, and comes out hot —ready to go.

Simply moving around is another way to jump-start your productivity. In its purest form, motivation is really just physiological arousal that incites you to action. You can learn to consciously crank up this arousal to keep your energy high.

Imagine you're having trouble staying awake as you try to read another coma-inducing inspection report. All you may need to do is get up and move around a bit. Try walking down the hall to get supplies, or take a quick stroll around the building. If it is a lunch hour, and you can take a longer walk or go the gym, even better. You may be surprised by how alert you feel when you return.

There's a good physiological explanation for why this works: When you exercise, your blood pumps faster so that more nutrients can be brought to your muscles and organs. At the same time, your breathing becomes quicker so that more oxygen can be delivered to your cells.

When you return to your desk after a walk or workout, your body and brain have received the nutrients they need to be replenished. The drowsiness, which probably was caused by the lack of enough oxygen getting to your brain, has been banished as well. All of this makes you feel more awake and alert and helps your brain function better.

ON THE STREET

Reprogram your motivation using the "Day One" name. Post a sign saying "Day One" in your office, or set up your computer to flash the words on the screen when you turn it on. Whenever you see the words, say them out loud several times, in a forceful voice, and imagine those first-day feelings of eager anticipation and excitement. Eventually, you will condition yourself to experience these feelings just by looking at the signs.

Locked-in interest. You can revive your energy by setting aside time and space to redirect your thoughts and behavior. Two techniques *time lock*, and *focal lock* can help.

In time lock, you block off a period of time anywhere from a few minutes to several hours for doing intense work. Tell other people in your office that you don't want to be disturbed and to hold your calls. Once you've made such a big deal about your intention, you'll feel as if you must put the time to good use. Don't make the time period any longer than you need. Otherwise, you risk feeling as though you're spinning your wheels again.

In focal lock, you prepare to make the best possible use of your time lock period. Write down a list of all the tasks to be accomplished during this time. Let's say you set aside an hour. You might designate it for making five phone calls and researching a neighboring community. This ensures that you don't waste your valuable block of time. As you cross off the tasks, it also reinforces your belief that you can be very productive when you set your mind to it. This, in turn, may help inspire you to be more focused and effective the rest of the time.

Before long, you'll probably notice that your energy and motivation are spiraling upward. After all, at the end of the day, nothing is more motivating than success.

All of the aforementioned self-motivational techniques are examples of how to use the components of your emotional operating system to get you to take care of business.

Your Mutual Motivation Estate

No agent is an island, and sometimes it helps to get a little motivational push from friends, family, and coworkers. You can develop a network of friends, family members, and colleagues to help you overcome setbacks or crises of confidence.

The players on your personal support team need to meet three basic criteria. They must be:

1. *People you trust.* Otherwise you won't feel comfortable turning to them for help.
2. *Available.* They can't help you if they're not around.
3. *Suitable.* Otherwise they won't be able to help, even if they want to.

The characteristics of a suitable motivator vary with your needs. Sometimes what you really need is a good listener, whereas other times you need someone who spoons up a mom-like dose of praise: "You're the smartest person in the office, and the hardest-working, too."

One of the main functions of your support team is to help you keep your emotional perspective when times are tough. Maybe you've just lost an important client and are feeling dejected. Your supporters can remind you that it was just one individual, and you still have more clients this year than last. Once you hear how other people see the situation, you might view it less emotionally and more rationally. In addition, you may regain your motivation to seek solutions to the problem. Share your ideas, and ask for input from your supporters. Soon you may realize that there really is a way out of your predicament. For instance, you might come up with ideas to attract enough new clients to more than replace the business you've just lost.

Keep in mind that any good relationship is a two-way street. Let your supporters know that the willingness to help is mutual. Show your friends and coworkers that you aren't merely a foul-weather friend. Call or visit when you don't have problems, just to say hello and ask how they're doing.

ON THE STREET

Think of four people whom you trust and who are fairly available to you. Put their names on an index card, and keep it on your desk. When you need a motivational push or support for a particular situation, give them a call. It will help.

Motivators Wanted: Dead or Alive

You can seek motivation from people you don't actually know but still admire. Your personal motivator can be alive or dead, real or fictional. You might pick a famous entrepreneur, a sports star, a figure from history, or a character from your favorite novel. Ask yourself what that person would do in your situation, or seek the person's advice in an imaginary conversation.

You may also think of specific moments in your hero's life that you found particularly motivating. Most likely, the thought of it will psych you up. One agent told me that every time he needed to get himself pumped up, he thought of a World Series in which his team came back from the brink of disaster. "I think of myself as part of that team, and it gets me going," he told me.

Rah-Rah Office Space

A third way to jump-start your productivity is to cultivate an environment that is conducive to success in the context of emotional intelligence—using outside stimuli to evoke motivation. Here's how to turn your workplace into an environment that makes you more productive.

- *Breathe clean air.* Nothing will get you yawing and nodding off faster than stale air that is depleted of oxygen. If you suspect that your office has a faulty ventilation system, contact your building management. Crack a window, if you can, or buy yourself a desktop air purifier. Then step outside during breaks for frequent infusions of fresh air.

- *Inhale the sweet smell of success.* Studies have shown that scents such as peppermint and citrus can enhance your energy and focus. Try plugging air fresheners into a nearby electrical outlet, or keep a little bowl filled with dried peppermint leaves or dried lemon rind on your desk.

- *Listen to soothing sounds.* Sound carries emotion. By emphasizing the right sounds and minimizing the wrong ones, you can decrease stress and increase motivation. If lively music works like a shot of adrenaline for you, try listening through your headphones while you read or do paperwork. On the other hand, if you spend your days listening to phones ringing, horns honking, and construction work on the floor below, try closing the door and using earplugs when you can. You can also try meditating to help tune out noise.

- *Work in good lighting.* Psychologists have found that some people lose their drive and become depressed when they don't get enough of the ultraviolet (UV) rays found in sunlight. Take advantage of natural light, letting the sunshine in during times of day when it doesn't blind you or create glare on your computer screen. If you don't have a window, try installing a UV bulb in your lamp or overhead lighting fixture.

- *Gather support objects.* Surround yourself with items that spark your enthusiasm —a photo of your child, an inspirational quote from your business idol, or your "Real Estate Agent of the Year" trophy, for example. You can also jot down inspirational quotations or notes on Post-its to keep yourself on track.

- *Clear off that clutter.* If you have trouble finding forms or phone numbers because they're buried under a mountain of paperwork, you'll probably find your energy waning. Vow that you won't go home until all those papers are in their proper files, those phone numbers are logged into the right database, and the top of your desk is in full view. Then keep things neat and user-friendly.

One last reminder: You can draw strength from supportive friends, inspirational heroes, and an energizing environment, but ultimately, it is up to you to make the best use of these resources. When it comes to your own motivation, you're always the one with the final control.

Turning Setbacks Into Comebacks

Unfortunately, even the best-laid plans don't always pan out. You may seem to be going along just fine, when suddenly —wham! —a setback sends you veering off course. Your forward movement comes to a grinding halt, and your motivation plummets. At such times, your self-esteem may crash as well, leaving you waylaid by feelings of fear, doubt, and hopelessness.

People respond to career setbacks differently. Most, however, experience setbacks as some type of loss —whether of direction, motivation, self-esteem, confidence, or pleasure in their job. Most also tend to go through the same stages associated with loss —disbelief, anger, wanting to turn back time, depression, acceptance, hope, and positive activity.

To regain your momentum, you must fully experience and move through each of these stages. You might experience several stages at once, or you might return briefly to a stage you've already passed. The only requirement is that you thoroughly work through each stage. This is where your *comeback toolkit* comes into play.

The tools you„ll need. It is not easy to deal with setbacks —they are emotionally arousing, draining, and taxing. The good news, though, is that you already have learned the skills that will help you turn a setback into a comeback. The key is to remember to use them. They include:

- Tuning in to feelings and thoughts
- Using motivational self-statements and constructive internal dialogue
- Keeping a sense of humor
- Practicing relaxation techniques
- Engaging in physical activity
- Using problem-solving methods
- Drawing from a support team
- Reassessing goals and setting new ones

Honing these skills gives you reliable tools that really work and make up your essential comeback toolkit.

Here's how the skills in your toolkit can help you move smoothly through each of the stages that characterize the setback process.

- *Disbelief:* The most common response to setbacks is disbelief— "I can't believe it," or "This isn't happening." At crisis points, however, denial serves as a valuable buffer by giving you time to compose yourself before the onset of powerful emotions. Eventually, of course, you'll need to tune in to your feelings and appraise your situation. But you can ease into this process gradually. Let's say that you've just learned that your top listing is being taken off the market. You might tell yourself, "I'm going to have to work extra hard to find new listings to take

up the slack. It is scary, because it is a tough time for business."
When such thoughts become too threatening, however, try
pulling a Scarlet O'Hara: "I'll think about that tomorrow." That
way, you'll experience negative feelings, but protect yourself
from being swamped by them.

- *Anger:* The next stage is usually resentment and hostility. You
  might find yourself thinking, "This is so unfair," or "That client
  always had it in for me." These thoughts can kick off a self-
  defeating cycle —you feel bitter and complain, which pushes
  people away, which just makes you feel more bitter and angry.
  Treat this kind of anger as a cue that something is wrong—that
  you need to rethink your situation to determine where you got
  off track. In the process, you'll often wind up reassessing old
  goals and setting new ones. You can also burn off some anger
  with physical activity or reduce your level of ire by using your
  relaxation techniques.

- *Yearning to turn back time:* At this point, you probably find
  yourself pining for the good old days, thinking, "If only I hadn't
  missed that call "or "If only September 11 had never happened."
  The best way to deal with a counterproductive nostalgia attack
  is to engage in a *constructive inner dialogue.* Ask yourself, "So
  what do I do now? How do I shift myself back into high gear?"
  Maybe you need to consider some fresh prospecting or marketing tactics. A little yearning for the past can prompt you to
  explore your options for moving forward in the future.

- *Depression:* This stage might be your toughest hurdle, since
  depression can create an overwhelming sense of hopelessness
  and inertia. The good news is that once you've made it through
  this phase, you'll find yourself over the hump and well on your
  way to a successful recovery. To help banish your blues, draw
  on your *support networks*—friends, family, and colleagues, who
  can help boost your motivation levels and keep you focused and
  positive. You might also try using motivational self-statements

such as, "I can do this," or "I'm a great financial agent, and I can convey that to clients."

- *Acceptance:* Reaching this phase means that you've made it over the hump. Your confidence is returning, and you know you've weathered the worst of the storm. Self-awareness can help you get in touch with your intentions. This, in turn, can help you focus on your new goals and plan a strategy for achieving them. If you want to attract new clients, for example, set your goal—say, developing a persuasive marketing letter—and then go for it.

- *Hope:* At this point, you're feeling downright optimistic. You've made it through the hard part without losing your sense of humor. You have a goal in mind, and you know the steps you'll need to take to achieve it. Your self-esteem is revitalized. This rush of hope gives rise to a burst of energy, which you can harness to carry into the next and final stage.

- *Positive activity:* Finally! You feel enthusiastic and ready to tackle whatever it takes to get back on track. Your motivation has returned full force. To convert your energy into effective action, try breaking down your goals into mini tasks. You might write a first draft of your letter, ask colleagues to critique it, write a revised draft, and so on. This is also the time to use your problem-solving skills to devise effective solutions for any snags that may occur.

Encountering a stumbling block can often fuel a dreaded catch-22: suffering a setback temporarily saps your motivation—motivation that, ironically, is precisely what you need to overcome the setback. If you find yourself stuck in this cycle, reach into that comeback toolkit. Drawing on these tools helps you mobilize your feelings, thoughts, and arousal to fight your way back, restoring your energy, confidence, and all-important drive to succeed. If you have been making the necessary investment, it is safe to say that your emotional intelligence property is beginning to develop and increase in worth. The next step in becoming an emotionally intelligent real estate agent is to learn how to incorporate your emotional intelligence into your relationships with your colleagues, assistants, and of course, your clients.

TWO

Increasing Your Property Value By Diversifying Your Emotional Intelligence

D IVERSIFYING your emotional intelligence means investing it in the work relationships that impact your bottom line—with your managers, team colleagues, and clients.

You can leverage your emotional intelligence in these bottom-line relationships in many ways, but to do so, you must remember to use what you have already learned.

For example, if your manager or a client criticizes you, to process their thoughts, you must manage your emotions so that you can make accurate appraisals and respond productively instead of defensively. If you are dealing with an emotionally aroused client, not only will you have to manage your emotions, perhaps by breathing slowly, but you must also remember to respond to the message of the emotion so that you can respond effectively and bring rationality to the encounter. If you want to tune in to your colleagues and team members, you will have to remember to practice your sensory awareness, and especially refrain from making appraisals without getting them documented. In other words, your intrapersonal emotional intelligence supplies you with many skills that affect your work relationships. Now, we can develop your emotional intelligence (EI) property by developing your *interpersonal expertise.*

INTERPERSONAL EXPERTISE

Interpersonal expertise refers to your ability to relate well to others. Building consensus, managing conflict, dealing with those who are emotionally charged, giving and taking criticism, and making meetings productive are all skills that are seeded and bloomed by your interpersonal expertise.

Interpersonal expertise boils down to two main factors:

- The ability to analyze a relationship so you can understand its goals and boundaries
- The ability to communicate so you can exchange information effectively with another person

You can be the smartest, most knowledgeable, and hardest working agent in your office, but if your interpersonal expertise falls short, so will your bottom line.

Can You Relate?

Before you can even start honing your interpersonal emotional intelligence skills, you must be aware of and understand three factors that impact all relationships: *needs, time,* and *communication.*

Relationship needs. People enter into relationships, first and foremost, to meet their needs. Ideally, a relationship is a mutually beneficial arrangement. Your relationship with a client, for instance, helps you make money and maintain your position at work, while it helps your client find a home —or sell his house at a profit.

ON THE STREET

Think of your relationships at work—your relationship with a particular client, a specific colleague, your assistant, your manager. Ask yourself (you may want to write it out) the following:

- What are my needs for each work relationship?
- Which relationships are meeting my needs and which aren't?
- How can I get my needs met from my work relationships?
- What are the needs of my manager, client, and colleagues?
- How am I doing in meeting their needs?
- How can I better meet the needs of my working relationships?

Emotionally intelligent real estate agents (EIRAs) are keenly aware of what they need from each of their work relationships. Armed with this information, they can begin to develop strategies on how to meet their needs.

EIRAs are also keenly aware of what others need from the working relationship. Armed with this information, they can begin to generate the actions that will meet the needs of others. Meeting the needs of others (and having yours met) promotes relationship longevity. With clients, it turns into referrals.

Relationship time. A relationship involves *ongoing* contact over time. If you see a client only when you have a showing, the two of you are likely to remain acquaintances. If you speak to the client frequently, even when you don't have a property to show, you'll have the opportunity to develop an actual relationship. By speaking with this client frequently, you'll gradually pick up clues about what makes him or her tick and get a much better sense of what type of home they will actually buy. As you build a rapport, you'll eventually see sides of the client's personality that were hidden from you before. Each conversation will provide fresh insights, which you can ultimately use to make future encounters as productive as possible.

Emotionally intelligent real estate agents are tuned in to the fact that they can improve their relationships by having *quality work relationship time.* When you have quality work relationship time — whether with your boss, clients, or assistant —you increase the chances of both parties having their needs met, thus perpetuating a productive relationship. This occurs because you communicate at a meaningful level, one in which both parties are free to express their *thoughts, ideas,* and *feelings.* Doing so promotes openness, genuineness, authenticity, trust, and a host of other factors that we all know make up the cornerstone of every good relationship.

Of course, it is impossible to communicate on a meaningful level if you don't spend time with the particular individual. This is why emotionally intelligent real estate agents are very high on "interaction" — they know that it is in their best interest to interact with those who influence their success. Thus, it is a good idea to think of ways you can spend more time with those who affect your success, as a prelude to promoting the quality of the relationship. As the quality of the relationship improves, you will find that your needs are being met.

Communication. Communication is essential in any relationship. Communication is *an exchange of information.* For example, you wouldn't say you have a relationship with the cashier who checks out your groceries at the supermarket once a week, unless you start trading gossip and news about your personal lives. Of course, negotiating this territory can be tricky when clients are involved, but the more emotionally aware you are, the better you can predict how a given statement about your feelings and thoughts may affect a particular client or colleague. This helps you share information in a way that is likely to serve your relationship well.

ON THE STREET

- *Increase your calls to clients.* Besides updating them, throw in a joke, and ask how they are doing. Add a minute or two to your conversations.
- *Spend a little more time with your assistant.* Ask about his or her goals, what he or she would like to do more of, what gives him or her trouble, how you can be helpful.
- *Always acknowledge your boss.* At every encounter, even if it is for a minute, say more than just a hello.

A crucial point is that there are many levels of information exchange. Indeed, when people say they are not communicating, it is often because they are using different levels of information exchange —one is on AM, the other FM.

To communicate effectively, you need to identify the various levels at which others are operating. Think of a team meeting where one person is exchanging pleasantries ("Nice weather, isn't it?"), another is stating facts ("Our profit margin is shrinking."), and a third is expressing feelings ("I'm really hurt by your attitude."). If team members continue to function at such different levels, they will be hard-pressed to accomplish much. To avoid a Babelesque scenario —one where co-workers are essentially speaking different languages —learn to recognize the current level of discussion, and tweak it accordingly.

The four most common levels of communication are:

1. *Niceties:* These are the automatic pleasantries you exchange with friends, acquaintances, and strangers alike. "How's it going?" for example. Niceties are valuable as social lubricants,

but the connections they forge are typically flimsy. They tend to elicit such rote responses as, "Oh, fine. You?" Keep an ear out for the occasional, more meaningful reaction, such as, "Actually, I'm having a rotten day." This is your cue to ratchet up the level of discussion and talk about what's really going on.

2. *Factual information:* Whether you're reporting the latest sales figures, charting the mortgage rates, or teaching colleagues a new computer program, you're often in the position of articulating cold, hard facts. Remember that facts can provoke dramatic emotional responses. Think about the heights of happiness or the depths of despair prompted by a sharp rise or dip in the housing market. At your next team meeting, notice the impact of facts on our coworkers. Suppose you're reporting to your team on the decline in house listings. If you observe beads of sweat forming on one agent's brow or fidgeting in his seat, you can fairly conclude that the news is causing him significant anxiety. (Of course, he might also be ill.) Use this insight to help him put his fears in perspective. For example, you might point out the trends suggesting a turnaround next quarter.

3. *Thoughts and ideas:* Sharing opinions and beliefs means taking a risk. Unlike facts, your thoughts and ideas are not right or wrong. As a result, expressing them requires that you make yourself vulnerable to, perhaps, an out-of-hand rejection or harsh criticism. Most people become defensive and experience bruised self-esteem when rejected or harshly criticized, so it is safer for them to stick to the facts and discussions about the weather. Unfortunately, this often causes their business to stall. Emotionally intelligent real estate agents are willing to make themselves vulnerable because they believe that one of the ways they create their success is by expressing their thoughts and ideas to their managers and colleagues, and certainly to their clients.

4. *Feelings:* When people share feelings, they experience even more emotional vulnerability than when they share thoughts. Talking about feelings is precisely the path leading to the closest and longest-lasting relationships. The trick is to identify which feelings are appropriate to reveal and when. Some feelings are best kept out of the workplace, —your sexual attraction to a colleague, for example. Others may be more acceptable, but only under the right circumstances. Talking about feelings might be quite helpful, for example, when your goal is to build trust or consensus within your team, or when you are trying to work out conflict or dealing with a dejected client.

Once you learn to identify the different levels of communication, start using your knowledge to build stronger relationships. The key is to *know what you need from each encounter and what level of communication you must use to get the task accomplished so the need can be met.* For example, if you want to know how a client feels about working with you, you have to get him to disclose his feelings—a risky communication. If you want to know how you can be more effective with your assistant, you will have to get her to disclose her thoughts. If you want to help work out a conflict in your team, you have to get people to disclose their thoughts and feelings —otherwise, the root of the issue will not surface. If you are looking for how the team is performing, you want the facts, not comments, about low morale. (Certainly, this information would be important, but at the moment, you want just the financial data.)

Many times, you'll want to shift from one level to another, either because others are operating at a different level, the current level is causing someone discomfort, or because the flow of information would be better served by temporarily forgoing thoughts and feelings for facts. *Until you shift people to the appropriate level of information exchange, you will be unable to relate effectively and unable to accomplish the task at hand.*

One way to facilitate this kind of shift is to craft *strategic questions*. These questions force the individual to respond at the appropriate level of information exchange.

Suppose a team member named Susan is talking about an upcoming showing of her new listing. She's giving a straightforward summary, —square footage, bathrooms, kitchen space, bedrooms —but her uncharacteristically jerky movements and halting speech seem to signal unspoken misgivings. To guide the discussion into feeling territory, ask a strategic question: "How are you feeling about the presentation?" Listen to the response. Many times, the person will respond with a thought —not a feeling —such as, "I think it is okay." If this is the case, follow up with something like, "I know you think it is looking good; I'm wondering, though, how you are feeling about it—excited, anxious?" You might also offer a statement about your own feelings and impressions: "I sense that you may be feeling a bit anxious." When one member of a group (or conversation) opens up this way, others often follow suit.

Another useful tactic is to *solicit feelings and thoughts directly by stating your need*. To do this, try using the introductory phrase, "I'd like to hear," as in, "I'd like to hear how you're feeling about the presentation," or "I'd like to hear your thoughts on this." Bear in mind that whatever approach you take, some people will resist your best efforts to shift communication to the thoughts or feelings level. In such cases, your best strategy may be to dig deeper into her avoidance of expressing thoughts and feelings. You might say, "It seems like it is a little hard for you to share your feelings with me. Is it something I'm doing? How do you feel about my asking you this?"

Consider the client who is recently divorced and now has to sell his home. As the conversation goes on, the client clearly grows more and more anxious. You not only hear this in his words ("I'm afraid to even think about what would happen if I have to pay a lot of alimony") but see it in his actions (faster breathing and nervous fidgeting).

At this point, the client's strong emotions threaten to swamp his ability to make good decisions. As a skillful communicator, you realize it is time to take the intensity down a notch or two. You move the conversation away from feelings to a discussion of thoughts, ideas, and facts, and by so doing, actually help the client perceive the situation more accurately with a sense of confidence that his situation is manageable, especially when there is little chance of him not being able to afford alimony payments.

Every situation is different, but here are some other circumstances where you might want to shift to a new level of communication:

- *Move to the facts level if someone is very angry or anxious.* This helps defuse the situation and put the anger in perspective. Once the other person calms down, it is easier to deal with the situation effectively.
- *Move to the feelings level if someone seems sad or hopeless.* Sometimes the other person will only show such feelings nonverbally (not smiling, looking away). By eliciting a discussion of these emotions, you can help the person find ways to alleviate them.
- *Stay in the facts or thoughts level if you want to solve a problem.* Intense feelings make it hard to think clearly.
- *Stay in the thoughts or feeling level if you want to build trust.* An open, honest exchange of thoughts, ideas, feelings, and attitudes can help you gain the other person's confidence and cooperation.

When both parties are on the appropriate level of information exchange to get their needs met or a task accomplished, then both are relating well. Your goal is to relate well in your work relationships.

Increasing your awareness of relational needs and identifying the appropriate level of information exchange to satisfy those needs will allow you to diversify your emotional intelligence into the three most important work encounters, all of which affect your bottom line. Indeed, it is a safe bet to say that whether you are in Los Angeles, New York, or Milwaukee, within the first hour of your day, you will interact with your team, your manager, and your clients, so it makes good sense to see how you can use your emotional intelligence to get greater benefits from these relationships by relating well.

Before the next team meeting starts, observe the different levels of information exchange being used. Ask yourself:

- What is the goal of the meeting?
- What level of information exchange is needed to accomplish that goal?
- How do I get the team to shift to an appropriate level of information exchange?

Your answers will make the meeting much more productive. Before your next client encounter, ask yourself:

- What is the goal of this encounter?
- What level of information exchange is needed to accomplish that goal?
- How do I get the client to shift to an appropriate level of information exchange?

Your answers will help make your next client encounter more productive.

USING EMOTIONAL INTELLIGENCE IN THE OFFICE

It doesn't take long to realize that while colleagues might not give you any houses to list, they sure can make it easier for you to get to, and deal effectively with, those who do. It might be a solid referral from your manager, or a great idea from a team member, or even a message given quickly and accurately to you by your assistant. Whatever the case, if you don't have good relationships with these folks, then you might as well follow some *Soprano* advice: "Forget about it."

Over the years, I have found many ways for real estate agents to leverage emotional intelligence in their relationships with their colleagues, staff, and boss. Two of the more powerful are: becoming an effective team communicator, and positively giving and taking criticism. When you become a better team communicator, you can strategically influence the meeting for the betterment of all. When you give and take criticism positively, you motivate, educate, and develop others as well as yourself. Mastering both of these skills requires applying your interpersonal expertise.

Emotional Intelligence and Team Communication

I'm sure you've attended team meetings that are absolutely electric. Everyone is charged up with ideas and enthusiasm, and the air is crackling with group energy. At the end, you leave feeling as if you and the other team members have come up with some creative and collaborative solutions to problems.

You've also been to team meetings that are more like experiments in sleep deprivation. You struggle to keep your eyes open as one person drones on endlessly, while everyone else is too lethargic or scared to say anything. You leave feeling frustrated, isolated, and unproductive.

The difference between the two scenarios is team communication. A little constructive give-and-take lets team members resolve stubborn problems, generate fresh ideas, and learn how to work together as a cooperative unit. If your institution is one of the many that is integrating the services it provides to its clients, it is likely that you will spend more and more of your time in team meetings. Good team communication skills are now essential to your job.

Emotionally intelligent real estate agents realize that they cannot control their team members, but they also realize they can positively influence the team meeting by applying their emotional intelligence in the context of team communication. Consequently, if you asked emotionally intelligent real estate agents how they leverage emotional intelligence to enhance team communication, they would say:

- *Be inclusive.* Talk to everyone when you speak. Don't keep your eyes locked on one particular person. Instead, seek input from everybody, occasionally asking different individuals, "What do you think?" The EIRA wants the team to *feel* like a team, so he or she looks to get everyone involved, thus maximizing group energy. The EIRA also recognizes that everybody has the *need* to be included —being inclusive helps this need be met and produces better team relationships.

- *Discourage dominance.* Don't let one person hijack the discussion. The group will benefit from hearing everyone's ideas. If necessary, politely ask, "What do others have to say about this?" The EIRA knows that some folks have trouble asserting themselves in the face of a dominant personality. Thus, by asking for their thoughts and feelings, the EIRA helps team members *self disclose* and *assert* their thoughts and feelings.

- *Show support.* Keep morale high by giving out the verbal equivalent of gold stars. For example, "That's a great idea," or "You've obviously put a lot of work into this." The EIRA promotes *positive feelings* to enhance team communication. Giving praise publicly not only gives recognition to the individuals and builds their self-esteem, but encourages others to risk expressing their ideas too. It is also important to show support when a team member is feeling down —to do this, you must be aware of the feelings of your team members.

- *Stay calm.* Some meetings have greater potential for emotional volatility than others. A routine agenda is not as likely to generate fireworks as one affecting people's job security or reviewing their work performance. Aim to keep the emotional tenor low-key, whatever the topic on the table. If things get tense, ask questions that lead the discussion into neutral territory for a while. If that doesn't work, suggest a break. Say, "Hey, there is a lot of enthusiasm here; let's take ten, and then we can pick it up again!" Note how the EIRA has taken advantage of the fact that both anger and enthusiasm share increased *physical arousal,* and thus frames the situation as people becoming enthusiastic rather than angry. By encouraging the team members to appraise the situation as enthusiastic rather than anger-provoking, the EIRA can preserve rationality, and at the same time promote positive feelings.

- *Pay attention.* Notice how each person participates and responds in the meeting. Who is being left out, hogging the floor, or developing hurt feelings? You won't know if you don't keep your eyes and ears open. The EIRA uses *sensory awareness* to enhance team communication. While others often interpret sensory data inappropriately, the EIRA checks the accuracy of appraisals by either *documenting* comments or asking other team members to document their observations. By taking responsibility for this action, the EIRA ensures that the team communication will be much more accurate.

- *Invite disagreement.* A yes-man or yes-woman isn't very valuable as a team player. Don't fall into the habit of appearing to agree even when you don't, just because it's easier. Also, if only one side of an issue is being examined, it might pay to occasionally assume the role of devil's advocate. The EIRA takes advantage of the fact that different people *appraise* events differently, and by seeking out different appraisals —information exchange at the thought level —he or she increases exposure to new ideas. Because these different perspectives have been invited, conflicts driven by ego and power struggles are minimized. Recognizing that people appraise situations differently exemplifies the practice of being aware of the needs of others.

- *Use self-disclosure.* This involves clearly stating what you personally think, feel, and believe. For example: "I think productivity might go up if we hired another secretary." "I feel uncomfortable with this approach." "I believe the market is ready to rebound." When you share this way in a group, you may inspire others to do likewise. If people still don't open up, try throwing out such questions as, "What do you think about this idea?" "How do you feel about this situation?" The EIRA knows the importance of exchanging thoughts, ideas, and feelings, and models the behavior and knows how to ask *strategic questions* that gently force others to respond on the communication level needed to get the job done.

- *Listen dynamically.* This involves not only hearing what someone else is saying, but also understanding, acknowledging, and responding to the emotional subtext. When in doubt, restate the speaker's message in your own words as a way of making sure that everyone is on the same page. If you think a team member is angry, deal with it by asking what is wrong, and then guide the team to problem solve. If you think a team member, or several members, are anxious, focus on what the uncertainties are and help the team prepare for them so confidence can be restored. The EIRA pays particular attention to all words, facial expressions, speech hesitations, and tone. These factors accompany the verbal expression and give a glimpse into the emotional landscape of the speaker. Of particular importance, the EIRA listens to the message of the emotion. This allows him or her to surface the underlying emotional currents that cause the meeting to flow in particular directions.

- *Be assertive.* Let's say you have a different view from the others. It is important to state your position clearly and persuasively, but without denigrating anyone else's opinions. Likewise, when another person is expressing a minority viewpoint, try to make sure that person gets a fair hearing. The EIRA remembers that he or she is just expressing thoughts and feelings, and therefore begins comments with subjective phrases such as, "I think," "In my opinion," or "I feel," rather than expressing thoughts as fact, which would be more likely to cause arguments, conflicts, and power struggles. The EIRA remembers that the *intent* of assertiveness is to express feelings and needs in an appropriate manner, and thus communicates in accordance.

Using your emotional intelligence in the context of your teams' will help you profit—now and in the future!

ON THE STREET

During your next team meeting:

- Practice inclusion by soliciting thoughts from all team members.
- Build positive energy by publicly praising team members.
- Use self-disclosure to model expression of thoughts and feelings.
- Help the team communicate effectively by documenting and asking others to document their observations.

Positive Criticism

Giving and taking criticism is one of the hardest tasks financial agents encounter. In fact, even when necessary, many of them shy away from giving it, especially if the criticism is directed to a client or to their branch manager. What about taking criticism? Again, most agents handle criticism poorly, especially when being criticized by their manager or a client. This is unfortunate because counterproductive responses to criticism almost always come back to haunt you.

However, if you apply your emotional intelligence when giving and taking criticism, you can transform it from a negative event into a positive motivational experience that boosts self-esteem and productivity.

In so doing, you enhance your effectiveness with those you work with, and this inevitably improves your bottom line.

Here are some tips that will help you diversify your emotional intelligence into the everyday event of giving and taking criticism, whether it involves your manager, colleagues, or team members. Note how different aspects of emotional intelligence come into play.

Befriend criticism. Making criticism positive begins by revisiting and managing your emotional operating system. How do you appraise criticism? If you appraise it as a negative, it is not surprising that you respond defensively or end up feeling dejected. In contrast, EIRAs appraise criticism as valuable information that increases their awareness about how they are doing and how they can do better. This appraisal helps them listen to the information being presented and to evaluate it on merit rather than emotional irrationality. Because EIRAs have a positive appraisal of criticism, they seek it out from their managers, colleagues, and clients. Befriending criticism helps the EIRA continually learn ways to become more effective. Befriending criticism increases your self-awareness.

Maintain a positive intent. Many times, the criticism we give or receive is destructive for the simple reason that we lose our *awareness about our intent*. Lots of criticism comes out of buried resentment, so the intent becomes to express anger and make the person feel bad. It is better to express your feelings of resentment and anger than hide them under the guise of constructive criticism. To give positive criticism, your intent has to be *improvement-oriented*—to make a situation better. With this intent in mind, you can begin to generate the behaviors and style of criticism that demonstrate your desire to help. One way to make your criticism improvement-oriented is to move the behavior you are criticizing into the future by emphasizing the next time. For example, "Hey Bill, *the next time* Mr. Jackson calls, let me know because I want to take his calls." This phrasing of the criticism communicates many psychological subtleties, such as confidence in Bill

(I trust you to do it better next time) and job security (If there is a next time, you know you are not getting fired).

Be timing-oriented. There's a time and a place for everything, criticism included. Sometimes, the best time and place for criticism is your office, other times the neutral conference center, and sometimes, you can just weave it into the natural flow of the conversation. Key questions to ask yourself to help you become timing-oriented include: Am I ready to give this criticism, and is the person ready to hear it? Is this the best place and time to give the criticism? Would I want to be criticized in this environment? One unsuitable time to give criticism is when you are not managing your emotions, especially anger. Not only will your anger quickly turn the encounter into a negative event, your recipient is also likely to blow off your observations, thinking that what you said was motivated by anger, not your rational thought.

Also, don't criticize a colleague or assistant who is angry; you will most likely be told, "I don't want to hear it."

ON THE STREET

- Write down a positive definition of criticism, and put it on your desk. For example, "Criticism is information that can help me grow," or "Criticism is teaching appropriate skills and knowledge."
- Write down three instructional self-statements that will help you respond productively when you receive criticism, such as, "Here's an opportunity to learn how my manager/client thinks," or "They are telling me how to do my job better."

Protect self-esteem. When criticism attacks the recipient's self-esteem, count on a defensive response. Putting people down is hardly a way to make them receptive to your thoughts. Avoid destructive labels and phrases such as, "That was really a stupid thing to do," or "You are so pig-headed." Also avoid making statements that are gross overgeneralizations: "You *never* give me my messages," or "You *always* interrupt me when I am with a client." Such statements are rarely true, so you can expect a defensive response when you use them. Try changing your *always* or *never* to *sometimes*. "Sometimes you interrupt me when I am with a client," stands a better chance of getting through because *sometimes* is true, whereas *always* or *never* isn't. Of course, if you manage your emotions, you will be less likely to use overgeneralizations and destructive labeling statements because you will have greater accuracy in your appraisals of the individual.

Put motivation into your criticism. "Hey, John, I'd like you to work a little harder in developing clients so I can make more money," will probably do little to motivate your assistant or partner. Don't be naive; people change for themselves, not for you. To produce results, the EIRA is clear on how responding to the criticism benefits the recipient. Sometimes the incentive is money, other times recognition, or it might be the opportunity to do something different. Practice motivational flexibility, and if one incentive doesn't work, try another.

Criticize strategically. You have a listing strategy for each of your clients. Do you have a *criticism strategy*? What do you want your criticism to accomplish? What is your criticism goal? How will you get the person to be receptive to your thoughts? How might he or she get defensive, and how will you overcome it? When and where is the best time to give the criticism? Ponder these questions before you give criticism. Take the time to formulate a strategy for what you want to say and how best to communicate it. Ask yourself: "How can I communicate this information so the person will be receptive?" "How can I communicate to my assistant that he needs better skills with clients who call?" "How can I communicate to my manager that she needs to be more open to my suggestions?" "How can I communicate to my fellow financial agent that his behavior in team meetings causes team distress?" Your answers will help you in creating an effective criticism strategy, and at the same time, often prevent you from giving criticism destructively.

Acknowledge that your criticism is subjective. In its purest form, criticism is an evaluation, so remember any time you give criticism that it is your subjective evaluation. Instead of making your criticism sound as though it is fact, preface your criticisms with subjective phrases such as, "In my opinion," or "This is what I think." Subjective phrases set the stage for transforming criticism from a one-way negative monologue into a dialogue—an information exchange of thoughts and ideas where the goal is to improve a situation. When you acknowledge that your criticism is subjective, you let recipients know that you are open to hearing their appraisals of events, and they are more apt to share their thoughts, especially if you ask for them. "These are my thoughts, and I would like to hear yours too."

Recognize when you are ineffective. Pay attention to emotional cues, such as facial expressions, body posture, or interruptions, which can tell you how your criticism is being received. If you note defensive behavior, rather than saying, "You're getting defensive," recognize *that you are being ineffective in your communication*. Take a deep breath, and try another approach.

Follow up. Sometimes it is an hour later, others times a day or two, but EIRAs check back with the recipient of criticism to see how he or she is doing, to give support, to make sure that the criticism was experienced as a put-up, not a put-down.

The Art of Criticism

The art of criticism means specifically identifying the criticism you want to give, and then packaging it, individualizing it, and stylizing it to the particular encounter. This means being creative, clever, and, most importantly, strategic.

Sometimes, the art of criticism can involve more than just verbal communication. One real estate agent told me that she couldn't stand the cigars that one of her clients smoked when he came to visit.

Every time he visited, which was fairly often, he would light up one of his big stinky cigars. The smell was terrible, and it was always noticeable to the client who came to visit later in the day. The agent said, "Because he gave me so much business, I wanted him to be comfortable and didn't want to offend him by saying anything. So the next time he came, I removed all the ashtrays from my office. It worked; he didn't light up. I don't know how long I can go without having ashtrays in my office, but at least it gives me some time to think of something else."

The point is that *you can give criticism in multiple ways, not just with your words.*

Other times, the art of criticism can take the form of a one-line statement. But whether it is behavioral, a one-liner, or a process over several weeks, strategic thinking must be used. How might the art of criticism sound in different scenarios?

I have heard many "how to criticize" questions from agents. Here are a few of the most common and difficult criticism situations they encounter —examples of how the art of criticism might be practiced on the first try with a just few lines, or even one line:

SITUATION: Criticizing a client who continually requests meetings but then doesn't show up or cancels at the last minute.

GOAL: To get the client to give appropriate notice if canceling and/or to get the client to come to meeting.

PHRASING: At the time the client schedules the next meeting, say: "Yes, Jack, I can show you the home tomorrow at 3:00. Do me a favor, please—call me an hour before, around 2:00, to let me know you are going to make it.

I understand that sometimes you get sidetracked and have to cancel—that's okay, but if I don't hear from you by 2:00, I will assume you are not coming, and no one will be there to let you see the house.

SITUATION:	Criticizing your branch manager for not being supportive.
GOAL:	To get your boss to help you by showing or implying how being supportive to you will help his bottom line.
PHRASING:	It is best to work this into the flow of conversation rather than making it a stand-alone conversation. Say something like, "You know, John, I've been doing a lot of thinking about how I can improve my performance, and I think I could greatly improve my bottom line if you would help me out by giving me a little more information."

SITUATION:	Criticizing a team member for being abrasive at team meetings.
GOAL:	To increase the team member's awareness of how she comes across so she can relate more effectively to the team.
PHRASING:	Right after the meeting in which the team member acted abrasively, approach her with subtlety. "You know, Gail, you may want to rethink how you are coming across at meetings. It may not be the way you want people to perceive you. I know that you are not abrasive, but when others hear comments like the ones you just said to Jane, what are they to think of you? I thought you might want to think about that."

What if you don't get positive results? What if the situation becomes repetitive and inevitably emotionally distressful? After all, there is no right way to deliver criticism, and there is no guarantee that the recipient will be open to what you are saying.

To generate more effective responses to repetitive and difficult criticism encounters, ask yourself these five questions:

1. *What is the goal of your criticism?* Once you know what you want your criticism to accomplish, you can begin to strategize about the way to deliver it.

2. *What makes the criticism difficult?* Sometimes the barrier is the relationship, such as your relationship with your manager or an important client. Sometimes it is the content of the criticism, such as the personal hygiene of your assistant or team member. Other times, it is a specific attribute of the recipient. Once you know what makes it difficult, you can begin to figure out how to make it less difficult.

3. *What have you already tried?* Awareness of what you have already tried will prevent you from continuing to be ineffective. In fact, any time you catch yourself saying, "I've spoken to you a dozen times about this," you know that you have been ineffective for a while.

4. *How would others handle the encounter?* If you don't know how to handle the encounter, ask someone else. Chances are great that one of your colleagues has had to deal with a similar situation. That colleague can help you brainstorm to come up with new responses.

5. *How can I communicate this information so the person will be receptive?* The bottom line is always to be strategic, to figure out how you can communicate the information —whether it is through your words, your actions, or even using other sources to legitimize your point t—in a way that will increase the likelihood that the recipient will be receptive to what you say and act on it.

ON THE STREET

Think of a criticism that you have to give to a client, team member, or assistant. Ask yourself:

- What do you want your criticism to accomplish?
- What specific information do you want to communicate?
- What is the benefit to the recipient?
- What is the best time to communicate the information?
- How can you communicate the information so that the recipient will be receptive to your message and act on it?

EMOTIONAL INTELLIGENCE AND CLIENT RELATIONSHIPS

Talking with Clients

Money may talk, but real estate agents are the ones who must communicate what it's saying. By using emotional intelligence when communicating with clients, you can observe the influence you're having on their feelings, thoughts, and behaviors, and adjust your message accordingly.

Imagine meeting with a client to discuss her housing priorities, suggest a particular house, or listen to a complaint. The wrong word or a misunderstood meaning can sink your relationship with the client. Effective communication skills, on the other hand, can spark a personal connection and forge a lasting bond. Among the most important emotional intelligence communication skills to hone are *self-disclosure*, which involves clearly telling the other person what you think, feel, and believe; *assertiveness*, which involves sticking up for your ideas and opinions while respecting the other person; and *dynamic listening*, which involves hearing what the other person is really saying.

Exposing Yourself

Self-disclosure is the term psychologists use for expressing your own thoughts, feelings, and beliefs. Not surprisingly, self-disclosure statements often begin with certain key phrases: "I think this might be a good investment strategy for you." "I feel more comfortable with this approach." "I believe this is a realistic listing." By tacking the little word *I* onto the front of these statements, you acknowledge that they are yours and yours alone. This lends some credence to your statements, because it shows that they are based on your personal experience. It also makes it clear that they are the opinions of just one person, leaving the door open for other, equally valid opinions, including those of the client.

Sometimes it is important to let the other person know not only what you think, feel, and believe, but also what action resulted from those thoughts, feelings, and beliefs. *Action statements* let the person know why you did, are doing, or will do, something. Let's say you promise to call a client's office at 9:00, but no one answers at that time, or at 9:10 or 9:20. By the time your client's assistant finally answers the phone and puts you through, it is 10:00. If you don't explain what happened, the client might assume you're calling late because you're unreliable or careless. By saying, "I tried calling a few times around 9:00, but didn't get an answer," you can prevent this misperception.

Asserting Yourself

Assertiveness is another big piece of the communication pie. It involves defending your rights, ideas, and opinions without denigrating those of the other person. This sets it apart from aggressiveness, which involves ignoring the other person's needs, and passiveness, which involves ignoring your own. When you assert yourself, you strike a balance that benefits both of you.

Let's say one client has a bad habit of showing up without an appointment and expecting you to drop everything to talk to her. Here are some ways you could use assertiveness to keep this from continuing:

- *State your position.* Tell the client that you value her business, but she still needs to make an appointment to see you.
- *Say it again.* Underscore your position by repeating it a few times, if necessary. Be consistent about what you want.
- *Give your reasons.* Explain that you need time to research, fill out paperwork, return phone calls, and accomplish other tasks that are crucial to the service you provide all your clients, including her.
- *Recall relevant facts.* If you already explained this to the same client last week, remind her about that conversation.
- *Watch your body language.* Sit or stand near the client, but not so close that you seem aggressive. Convey your determination by sitting or standing up straight and maintaining direct eye contact.
- *Control your tone of voice.* Speak in calm, confident tones. Don't let your irritation with the client turn up the volume.
- *Acknowledge her viewpoint.* Let the client know you understand her position that she should have access to you.
- *Look for a compromise.* Suggest that the client use e-mail when she has a quick question that isn't highly time sensitive or confidential. This lets you respond whenever you have a few extra minutes.

Dynamic Duos

Dynamic listening is yet another key part of the emotional intelligent communication process. Listening with emotional intelligence is more than just hearing what the other person is saying. It involves understanding, acknowledging, and responding to the emotional subtext beneath the words. To do this, you must become aware of how the other person's statements are filtered through your own feelings, thoughts, beliefs, and attitudes.

Consider a client who calls and says, "Something has come up, so I have to cancel our appointment on Thursday, but I'd like to talk to you when I get back in town next week." If you are naturally a glass-half-empty kind of person, you tend to register only the worst of what was said. And because this client was passed down to you by a second-rate predecessor, you have a tendency to regard him as a poor prospect anyway. All you hear the client saying is that the appointment is canceled. You don't hear him express his interest in talking to you when he can. As a result, you may miss a chance to follow up next week.

In this case, you might have heard the message more accurately if you had been more tuned in to your predilection to pessimism and your preconceived bias against the client.

Here are other ways to improve your listening skills:

- *Restate what you've heard.* Put the speaker's statements into your own words, and then repeat them back to him or her. This lets you check whether the message you received is, in fact, the one the speaker meant to send.
- *Clarify feeling statements.* When someone expresses a feeling, it often helps to respond with an "I hear" statement, such as, "I hear that you're concerned about the risk of losing your investment." Such statements reassure the speaker that you understand and care about what he or she is feeling.
- *Use acknowledgment phrases.* Comments such as "I see," "I understand," and "That's interesting," let the speaker know you're awake, alert, and on the same page. This is vital feedback for the other person to have.
- *Use body language.* This makes the same point as acknowledgment phrases, but with nonverbal cues. To show you're listening and understanding, give appropriate eye contact, and nod your head when you want to communicate agreement or encourage the speaker to continue to self-disclose.

Communication Lines

If you want clients to put their money where their mouth is, good communication skills are essential. The advice that one client might see as a welcome soft sell, another might view as too wimpy and vague. The approach that one client might see as reassuringly professional, another might view as formal and distant. Dynamic listening can help you dig beneath the client's words for the true feelings that underlie them. In a world where one size of advice doesn't fit all, this information can help you tailor your message more effectively.

Nowhere is this more important and more essential to your success than when responding to emotionally charged clients.

Emotionally Charged Clients

Emotionally charged clients call you when they experience an emotional reaction that causes them to question your performance, listing strategy, or general client service. Sometimes, it is to express anger and disappointment over your performance; other times it is out of anxiety and fear as they watch their house value plummet. Regardless of the emotion, the task of the emotionally intelligent real estate agent is to *emotionally mentor,* to respond in a way that helps the clients keep their emotions in perspective so that they can make the best decision, one that is driven by rationality rather than emotionality.

This is not to say that the clients' emotions and feelings are not appropriate. Indeed, most people we know would be angry and disappointed if their real estate portfolio dropped endlessly. However, *your clients—like most people—often mismanage their emotions.* So the emotional perspective they use to call on you is typically filled with distorted thinking, blaming communications, and a tendency to make impulsive choices. While it might be true that a client is best served by selling their property with you, you want the decision to be based on thoughtfulness, not emotional impulsiveness.

How do we know if clients are emotionally charged? They might say something like, "I'm angry that you didn't suggest to sell my property" Other times, we must be aware of their emotional cues—tone of voice, facial expressions, rate of speech, body gestures—but these emotional cues only aid us in a face-to-face encounter. The fact is, most agents hear the emotionally charged client on the telephone—the major means of communication between real estate agents and clients. So the prime way you will be subjected to the emotionally charged client is by his or her spoken statements—statements that are filled with emotions that blame, challenge, and express disappointment. *These statements encapsulate the emotions that the client is experiencing.*

Whatever the emotions expressed, these moments are defining client-relationship moments. If you apply your emotional intelligence, you can respond to the emotionally charged client in a way that builds trust and credibility —two factors necessary for developing and maintaining long-term client relationships. Responding ineffectively is a pretty good way to cause clients to take their business elsewhere.

Responding to Emotionally Charged Clients

The ability to respond effectively to the emotional states of clients is a hallmark of the emotionally intelligent real estate agent. It is not a daunting or stressful task if you follow the four steps below, all of which bring your emotional intelligence skills into action.

1. *Identify active emotions.* The prerequisite to responding effectively to emotionally charged clients is being aware of the emotions in play. Sometimes this is obvious, as when clients state their feelings. For those times when clients just launch into their verbosity, ask yourself, "How would I have to *feel* to say this to my agent?" Your answer will help you tune in to the emotions being presented. As to your own emotions, depend on your self-awareness to identify how you feel when

the client speaks to you. Usually, the emotions evoked in you by the client's statements are the same that are fueling the client to call.

2. *Determine what these emotions signal and how you will manage them.* To respond effectively to emotionally charged clients, it is crucial to understand the message of the emotions—theirs and yours. Once you understand the message of the emotions, you can determine how to manage them in yourself and how to respond in a way that returns the client's emotional perspective to a state that is reality oriented. As a refresher, here are the most common emotions that prompt clients to call you and what they communicate:

   - *Anger* communicates that something is wrong.
   - *Anxiety* communicates uncertainty.
   - *Fear* communicates the perception of threat.
   - *Disappointment* communicates being let down.
   - *Enthusiasm* communicates excitement.

3. For the most part, *taking charge of your thoughts, staying relaxed,* and *dynamic listening* will be the most effective ways to keep your emotional perspective when your client is charging at you. Keeping your own emotions in perspective will allow you to focus on your response strategy.

4. *Set up a strategy for responding.* What do you want your response to accomplish? For example, if you detect that the client is angry, part of your response strategy should be to minimize blame, as clients who are angry tend to blame their agent. If you feel that your client is anxious, part of your response strategy should be to say something that reduces the client's feelings of uncertainty. Generate your response strategy by asking yourself, "What do I want to say that responds to the

message of the emotion?" "How will I restore proper emotional perspective to the client?"

5. *Put into words an emotionally intelligent response.* What are the *exact words* you need to say to implement your strategy?

Like anything, mastering emotional mentoring takes a little time, but as your awareness grows, it will become easier and easier. Inevitably, your emotional operating system habituates the steps, causing automatic thinking that generates an emotionally intelligent response to an emotionally charged client every time one calls, whether he is angry, anxious, disappointed, fearful, or irrationally exuberant.

Here are some examples of how emotional mentoring might work with the five most common emotional states that prompt clients to call and throw a few emotionally charged statements at you. Remember, there is no correct response, so think about how you can make the model responses even more effective for you.

The angry client: When clients are angry, they believe they have been wronged. Their communication is filled with blaming accusations. Usually accompanying anger is fear. The clients not only believe they have been wronged, but also that there is a threat, in this case to their financial solvency. Emotional perspectives driven by anger and fear often cause the client to call and say, "What's going on? There hasn't been a showing in weeks! Why aren't you creating interest?"

- *Active emotions:* Anger, fear.
- *Information communicated:* Something is wrong; there is a threat.
- *Response strategy:* Validate the feelings of anger, reduce the perception of threat, minimize blame by building trust and cooperation, and help the client regain a perception of control.

- *Response implementation:* "Well, I'm angry too, and believe it or not, I'm even angrier that your house isn't selling." The words "angry too" validate the client's emotions by implying that you know the client is angry. "My job is to sell your house, not simply keep it listed for years." *Clarifying and stating positive intentions reduce anger.* "Can you imagine if my intent was never to sell your house? I think I could keep it on the market forever!" *This statement could be effective because it uses humor to exaggerate that your intentions are not to cost the client money. However, its effectiveness will be a function of your style and the quality of your client relationship.* "All right, listen, how about if we take a look at where we are—sometimes a team loses and makes no changes—and see what actions we might take." *The strategy behind this statement is to make the relationship cooperative, thus reducing the tendency to blame in the future. Promoting shared responsibility and a problem-solving-oriented relationship is the goal. Note the instruction to the client to listen.* "Six weeks with no showings seems like a long time, but it is still below industry average, so you might want to keep that in mind." *This statement puts the performance in a realistic perspective. Anger often creates exaggerated negative perceptions about the reality of the situation. By putting the performance in perspective, anger is dissipated, and a realistic appraisal of the performance can be achieved, which still might be anger-provoking but manageable, because it is at a more appropriate level in the context of the situation.* "So let's get started and see what we need to do to generate interest!" *This positive, action-oriented statement creates motivation and helps make the client relationship productive.*

The anxious client: Anxious sellers call when they feel unsure whether their house is going to sell. Anxious buyers call to see whether the deal is going to close. Usually, the client calls for reassurance that everything is okay. Frequently, there are also underlying feelings of frustration, as the client feels no progress is being made. The anxious client does not know what action to take, and says to you, "What should I do?"

- *Active emotions:* Anxiety, frustration.
- *Information communicated:* Uncertainty of actions to take; not attaining goals.
- *Response strategy:* The goal is to reduce anxiety by making the client feel more certain that the strategy for selling is a good one. Because the client is coming to you with lots of uncertainty, the call is also an opportunity to build trust. Provide information so that the client can see the actions taken are appropriate, thus reducing the need to feel uncertain about the prescribed course of action.
- *Response implementation:* "Well, I am pleased that you trust me and respect my opinion. I know I always feel better when there is someone I can trust to help me. Let's look at some market data to base our listing/buying on so we can meet our goals." *Data reduces anxiety. Note how you can take advantage of the client's asking what to do by reframing it as a belief and respect of your opinion. Disclosing to your client that you feel better when you believe your advice is trusted implies that the client trusts you as his or her agent.*

The disappointed client: Feeling as though you have let them down is the emotional perspective that drives disappointed clients to give you a call. However, disappointment typically blends into anger. After all, someone has to be blamed for the house not selling or the financing falling through, and it is not going to be the market or the bank; it is going to be you! Often, disappointed people avoid taking responsibility for their predicaments, thus causing them to feel victimized. What do people do when their disappointment is colored with anger? They look to take some action that will make things better, like getting a new real estate agent or prematurely lowering the price of their house. This is why disappointed clients often say, "I really feel I should find a new real estate agent."

- *Active emotions.* Disappointment, some anger.
- *Information communicated:* Unmet expectations, let down, blame.
- *Response strategy:* Redirect "feeling" into a "cognitive assessment" of the situation that will put it into a realistic perspective, *as disappointment usually stems from unmet expectations, which are often unrealistic.* A client who expects a 15 percent profit will be disappointed with 10 percent. That's why it is important to remember to *constantly clarify client expectations.* Because the client is communicating on a feeling level, respond on a feeling level first, then shift the client to "think" about expectations, rather than "feel" them, as the client will be less resistant to a thinking level than a feeling level.
- *Response implementation:* "Well that would hurt, but that is your choice." *Disappointment often causes feelings of helplessness. This statement restores a sense of empowerment by letting clients know that they are in control of the choices they make, thus subtly getting them to realize they are not a victim. It is their choice, and they are responsible for the consequences.* "I'm disappointed, too, and also frustrated. My goal is to sell your home at fair value, not below value." *Acknowledging that you, too, are disappointed conveys empathy, and the clarification of positive goals will help dissipate the client's tendency to blame you.* "I respect your feelings." *Instead of telling the client, "You shouldn't feel that way," you are validating the client's feelings, thus alleviating the need to keep expressing that disappointment.* "What do you think is the best thing to do?" *This part of the response helps the client move to a cognitive assessment of what to do, rather than ruminating in disappointment.* "You can tell me to lower the price now, or you can think about it. If you

want to lower it or take it off the market, let's come up with a plan. I don't want to be impulsive. On the other hand, if you decide not to lower the listing price, then we should reexamine market data and make sure that the house is listed correctly so we stand a good chance of meeting your expectations." *In the end, clients will do what they want, and you show them that the choice is entirely theirs. Telling them you don't want them to be impulsive communicates that you are looking out for their best interest. Reassessing their investments will give you a chance to clarify their expectations and make them more realistic, so that future bouts of disappointment in your performance can be minimized.*

The irrationally exuberant client: These clients call you because their irrational exuberance colors their perceptions to the point that they think their house is listed too low, the showings will only increase, and thus create a bidding war. Their exuberance makes them want more. While it is nice to have enthusiastic clients, they can be dangerous, especially when the bubble bursts, as their enthusiasm will turn to anger, directed at you. The key to handling these clients is to return their perspective to reality, and at the same time, take advantage of their positive feelings by getting them to give you more referrals. You have the opportunity to do this when they call and say, "We are getting a lot of showings. There is great interest. I want to raise the price!"

- *Active emotions*: Enthusiasm, pleasure.
- *Information communicated*: Excited, trusting, expectations exceeded.
- *Response strategy*: Take advantage of their "positive affect" by asking for referrals and more business. It can also be a smart move to tone down client enthusiasm by pointing out that there are always market conditions, independent of your abilities, that affect performance, and right now, these conditions

are favorable. What would be the rationale for this response, which is best said after you get referrals?

- *Response implementation:* "Thank you. I appreciate you telling me! It really makes me feel good." *Praising clients for praising you is sure to increase the chances that they will praise you in the future. You are also exchanging information on the feeling level, and this helps solidify trust.* "You know, you wouldn't believe how many homes I am showing, but let's remember that lots of showings does not mean people are going to buy or that you should raise the price. In fact, one of the reasons we are getting a lot of showings is because the listed price is correct. Raising the price might result in fewer showings, and as a result, lose a lot of buyers. If the price is too low, buyers will bid it up, so we really don't have to raise the price for you to get more. Remember, it is my job to make sure we are realistic." *Explaining to the client that he can still get more money without raising the price will keep him enthusiastic and also prevent him from being irrational and making a bad decision. These statements remind the client to think things through realistically.*

The fearful client: Fearful clients come in all types of houses. Whether they are selling or buying a mansion or a buying their first home, they have an emotional perspective that sees a house as something they might not be able to afford or resell. Because anxiety is well connected to fear, their communications are marked by many questions, and they are very slow to take action. Their fear keeps them stuck, which for you means a lack of business. Minimizing their fear so they can start to put some money on the table is the key. Fearful clients often tell you, "I do not want to buy a house I can't afford or need to put a lot of work into."

- *Active emotions:* Anxiety, fear.
- *Information communicated:* Uncertainty, threat of loss, lack of trust.

- *Response strategy:* Label the emotions/feelings so you can help clients manage them. Validate their feelings, present data to reduce anxiety, clarify intentions, and minimize the threat of loss.
- *Response implementation:* "Listen, nobody wants to lose money on a house or buy one they can't afford, and everybody feels some concern about the house they buy, just like a car, or even a new suit." *This statement helps you reframe fear into concern—a more tolerable feeling— and also makes the point that concern comes with any investment. By mentioning a car, and suit, the statement also implies that the client has already made numerous purchases.* "What I want to show you is how I can help you purchase a home with a risk level that you feel comfortable with and think is appropriate."

ON THE STREET

Think about statements you've heard that were driven by the emotional state of your clients—for example, anger, anxiety, dejection, or enthusiasm.

Your task is to walk through the process for reacting to this statement in an emotionally intelligent manner. To respond to an emotionally charged statement: Identify the emotions you feel when hearing this statement.

- Determine how you will manage your emotions productively.
- Identify your client's emotions.
- Determine what these emotions signal.
- Determine a response strategy.
- Implement a response.

This statement is useful because it communicates your positive intent to help them without taking them out of their comfort zone. "As I said, nobody wants to buy a home they can't afford, but my fear is that it will be harder to afford a home if you wait." *This is an ingenious statement that takes advantage of the person's fear by pointing out that if they do not buy, their fear of not being able to afford a home in the future might become a reality.* "Let's go over your finances, and I will show you some homes you can afford and will probably increase in the not too distant future." *This statement allows you to start the home-buying process, with the reiteration that there is no need to be fearful.*

There are many other emotionally charged statements that encapsulate the same five emotions, so the idea is not to memorize a particular response, but rather, to focus on the strategies being used for a respective client's emotional state.

THREE

Emotional
Intelligence In Action

I T'S NOT A DEAL until the check is cashed. So true! Ask any real estate agent, and he or she will quickly agree that a deal can fall apart any time, even after you have had your client accept a very good offer.

Sometimes, the deal breaker is based on the buyer's poor credit rating. Other times, it is a disastrous house inspection causing irrevocable differences. Sometimes, it is an unexpected family event. Whatever the reason be, it kills your commission.

While it is impossible to guarantee that the real estate process—from listing to closing—will go as hoped and scheduled, it *is* a guarantee that if you apply your emotional intelligence throughout the process, you tip the scales in your favor and increase the likelihood that you will end up with commission in hand.

THE REAL ESTATE PROCESS

Selling or buying a house might happen in a flash, but the fact is, there is a predictable process that leads up to signing the contract. Specifically, I've found there are six steps that are common to every real estate deal, and the emotionally intelligent real estate agent performs each extraordinarily well for the obvious reason that he or she is applying emotional intelligence skills in the context of each step. I have listed the goal, EI competencies, and EI skills you need to apply..

1. Finding Listings

GOAL: Identify potential listing opportunities
EI COMPETENCIES: Self-motivation and interpersonal expertise
SKILLS: Self-time lock, focal lock, interpersonal communication

You can't start earning your commission until you have a house to sell, and calling "Ghostbusters" is not going to help you find one.

The real estate process starts with increasing your awareness of potential listings, with the ultimate goal of getting home sellers to give you the rights to listing their homes. In today's market, this is a tough opening task, but your EI competencies of self-motivation and interpersonal expertise will make it easier.

Finding listings isn't the most glamorous part of your job. It takes a lot of energy and can also be boring. Time lock and focal lock can help you.

Implement time lock by blocking off a specific time period each day, with the essential requirement that you are unavailable to your colleagues, family, and yes, even your clients. The lone exception is emergencies, but you must define what constitutes an emergency; otherwise, you will be continually interrupted.

Remember, the function of time lock is to give you a specific amount of uninterrupted time so you can increase your concentration on a specific task. That means no phone calls, checking e-mails, or getting a cup of coffee. Once you do any of these activities, your concentration is broken, and the time lock is defeated.

Once you have your time lock period, you need to focal lock—identify a specific task that will fill the time lock period. In this step, it is the task of identifying and looking for potential listings. If you get an important phone call, forget it—you're in a time lock. Remember, one interruption can derail the entire time lock period and leave you with the feeling that you got nothing accomplished.

The actual act of getting listings is one of the most difficult tasks a real estate agent must perform, and yet it is crucial to being successful. There are no sure ways to get a listing, but here are some proven strategies that eventually will yield you results:

- *Ask for referrals.* This is probably the best way to obtain a listing. You have several sources to try. First, ask your friends. Let them know you are always looking for listings and, "If you know anybody who is thinking of selling their house, I'd appreciate it if you refer them to me. Thanks." Naturally, the closer the friend, the better the friendship, the more likely you are to get a solid referral.

  Next, spend your time lock period by phoning your past clients and other professionals, especially divorce lawyers and accountants. If your past clients are still living in the area, the purpose of your conversation is see how they are doing, and tell them, "If you have any friends that I can offer the same services I performed for you, please give them my name. Thanks." Of course, you only call past clients a few times a year.

  A third referral source is other professionals who are in contact with individuals who might be selling their homes, such as divorce lawyers and accountants. Here, your time lock is filled with phone calls to these individuals. To those you know, you might say, "Hey, if you have any clients who need to sell their house, please send them my way, or ask them if it would be okay if I gave them a call. Thanks."

For those you don't know, you could say, "Hi, I'd like to introduce myself. I'm a real estate agent and specialize in helping individuals and couples who need to sell their home quickly at a fair price. I always come in contact with many individuals who are selling their home because of divorce and are looking for a good divorce attorney. I'd love to have lunch with you so we can learn about each other's practice."

Crucial to asking for referrals is your comfort level. If you are uncomfortable asking any of the aforementioned sources for referrals, you are probably adhering to the erroneous belief that successful real estate agents do not ask for referrals. If you believe this, you will severely handicap your success. The fact is, successful real estate agents do ask for referrals, and furthermore, they feel comfortable in doing so. Mentally rehearsing the action might help you feel more at ease, as well as examine the basis of your assumption, so you can see its irrationality.

- *Use Internet marketing.* A second action to fill your time lock period with is Internet marketing. Here, you commit your time to finding listings by developing your Internet savviness. There are plenty of real estate websites that can lead to securing listings, but it takes time to find them and learn how to exploit them. You need to create that time by time locking and using focal lock to canvass the Internet.

- *Create presentations.* You will find it useful to block out several hours a month for the purpose of preparing and delivering presentations. You'll have to find a venue, promote it, and most importantly, make it fun and interesting with the goal being to let your potential clients know you are an expert in selling homes. Of course, you should vary the real estate topic monthly as a means to build your audience. It will only be a matter of time before someone approaches you at the presentation's end and says, "Hey, I'm getting ready to sell my house, and I'd like to list it with you!"

There are many other ways to identify listings, but their common denominator, like the aforementioned strategies, is that they all require effort and time. Applying your self-motivation through time lock and focal lock will help you identify the listings you seek.

2. Finding Clients

GOAL:	Represent buying clients
EI COMPETENCIES:	Self-motivation, interpersonal expertise
SKILLS:	Time lock, focal lock, assertiveness, listening, creating optimism and confidence, trust building

You can still make a living if you have no houses to list; you just have to have clients who want you to help them buy a home. In short, "Do you know anyone who wants to buy a home?" If the answer is "No," then you have to find them.

Your methodology and tools are similar to those you use to find listings. Some tips for procuring clients include:

- *Time lock an hour or two a day*, and simply identify all your sources that might be able to feed you referrals, such as accountants, lawyers, and financial agents. Spend your time cultivating these lists with phone calls, lunches, and visits to their office.

- *Meet with referral sources.* You won't have a lot of time to sell yourself, so make sure you are well prepared. Manage your emotions and pressures surrounding the situation by reminding yourself that you will have dozens of chances to sell yourself. Using your relaxation response will also help you come across as a confident professional. Importantly, use your self-awareness to make sure you assert yourself and directly ask for referrals. You might say, "Well, if you know anyone who is looking for a home, I'd love to meet with them so I can show them how I can help them."

- *Use presentations.* The key to an effective presentation is not spitting out rehearsed information, but rather, identifying the needs of the group you are speaking to and showing them how you can meet those needs. Assert your intentions, and do some hard listening. For example, "I'm here to answer your questions and concerns about buying a home, so please feel free to ask away," might be an opening statement. Capitalize on using all their senses by having some visuals but use them sparingly as this is not a corporate presentation. Create positive affect by having some tasty treats, perhaps having your business cards next to the trays of cookies and bowls of candy, or a carrot or two for the healthy.

- *Use the Internet.* Having your own website can be a powerful means for getting clients, but make sure it is attractive, and simple for people to find, and understand how you add value to their home shopping. Spending a few bucks on a consultant to help you maximize this effort is worth it.

- *Engage in Starbucks sessions.* Always Be Looking (ABL) for clients. Next time you are at Starbucks, practice your eavesdropping skills and conversation busting. If you keep your ears open, you will hear many people talking about house shopping. Your interpersonal expertise will help you enter their conversation, and before it ends, you have a client or a referral.

- *Immunize yourself to rejection.* Building a practice is not easy, so prepare for rejection, especially in today's market. Manage your rejection effectively by using your self-awareness. Tune in to your self-statements, and make sure they are not self-defeating. Avoid negative statements, such as, "I'm a loser; I'm never going to get any clients; I shouldn't be in this business." Instead, substitute these distorted thoughts with, "I know I will be successful; It takes time to build a practice; I will learn from rejections; I will do better tomorrow."

- *Practice problem-solving.* Think of a problem as an ineffective response. The fact that you don't have clients is not the problem. The problem is how you are looking for clients. In other words, focus on how you can respond differently, and find new actions to take. This line of thinking will help you generate novel ways of finding clients and bring a sense of confidence, optimism, tenacity, and enthusiasm to your efforts.

Pretty soon, you will have to hire an assistant!

3. Meeting With Clients About Listing Their House

GOAL: To get the listing

EI COMPETENCY: Interpersonal expertise, self-motivation

SKILLS: Establish trust, inspire confidence, self-disclosure, assertiveness, give criticism, create optimism, and tenacity.

First, know that meeting a client to obtain a listing can be a pressure situation, so reduce it immediately with your internal thoughts, by saying, "This is one of many chances. If I don't get it, there will be hundreds of other opportunities." The fact is, when we think of an event as being very important or as a singular opportunity, we increase psychological pressure, which impedes our performance by causing us to choke in the moment. Thus, your anti-choking strategy is counterintuitive. You must minimize the importance of the meeting and remind yourself you will have multiple opportunities to get other listings.

The most obvious reason for you to get listings is so you can earn your living. The fact is, you can have access to a thousand listings, but if you can't get one, you are not going to make money. Furthermore, unless you are selling your own home, you can't guarantee you will get any listing.

However, applying your emotional intelligence in the form of *interpersonal expertise* dramatically increases your chances of leaving the meeting with the client's commitment that you are his or her agent, which is the goal of this step.

Start applying your EI as soon as you meet your client by increasing your awareness to your posture so you appear confident. Standing up straight, smiling, and offering a firm—not strong—handshake, and good eye contact, will not only look confident, but through the process of emotional contagion, will transfer feelings of confidence to your client. In just a few seconds, you will create a positive atmosphere. In short, *act as if* you are a winner!

If you don't already know the client, or if he or she is not a friend, reiterate *your intention* for the meeting: "I'd like to be the listing agent for the sale of your house and tell you how I think I am suited to help you sell it." Naturally, you can express your intention in your own words, but be sure to be very clear.

Be a good listener by asking the client about his expectations, including asking price, what he will actually take, and his time frame for selling. Gathering this information will help you determine realistic expectations and give you data for future negotiations with the client and potential buyers.

Now, utilize your *assertiveness* by disclosing your *thoughts*. Begin by presenting your *critique* about the house, both pros and cons. Keep your critique positively toned, as most sellers will be offended if you only point out the flaws of their dwelling. Include your suggestions on how you think the client can stage the property to make it more appealing, and offer your thoughts on how he might be able to make the house even more sellable by spending a few bucks for cosmetics.

Don't give a soft soap job. This is important because your critique will be the basis of your suggested listing price. Help your cause by doing your research so that you can give the client a picture about the current market and its trends, competitive properties in the area, their listing price, and the actual selling price if they have sold. Conclude by stating what you think is a realistic listing price, one that will be attractive in the context of the client's time frame for selling. Many real estate agents make the huge mistake of not being prepared, and this is a turnoff to the client. The more prepared you are, the more the client will perceive you as an expert and able to successfully sell their property.

After you have asked for his or her thoughts about your critique, use your confident voice to explain your marketing strategies, ranging from advertising, Internet, showings, and any other marketing tools you think will be effective. To add color, tell some of your selling success stories. Be sure to reiterate the data that indicate a realistic expectation for the time it will take to make a sale.

Once again, ask the client for questions, and if there are none, it is time to complete the step by saying, "Well, if you feel comfortable with me and believe I will do the job you expect, I would love to make your property my listing. I am very confident that I can meet your sales expectations."

If you have followed the aforementioned guidelines, there is a very good chance the client will say yes. If not, it is only natural that you feel disappointed. Here is where self-motivation comes back into play in the form of dealing with adversity. Too many real estate agents interpret the rejection with these thoughts: "I'm a loser, I'm a failure, I should not be in this business." These thoughts make the rejection a personal failure, and frequently using them leads to a decline in performance.

Rather, your thoughts will serve you better if you think, "Okay, I failed in this situation. I can't get every listing. What, if anything, could I have done differently that would have gotten better results?" In other words, EI real estate agents use the rejection as a learning experience for their next effort, and in so doing, do not let the rejection lead to dejection; instead, they use it to self-motivate for the next meeting.

4. Dealing With Lots of People at an Open House

GOAL: To stimulate interest
EI COMPETENCIES: Self-awareness, interpersonal expertise
SKILLS: Listening, receiving criticism, creating positive
                    affect; individual recognition, follow-up

There is no better way to introduce your listing to the agent community than the "Open House," an event in which numerous agents, —often a dozen or more, —will trot through the home you are trying to sell. Assuming a market-based listing price, a good showing motivates the visiting agents to show it to their clients.

How can you apply your EI to maximize this event? Begin by assuming that the agents are all emotionally intelligent. This means that they will be turned off if you are pushy, try to "sell," or are intrusive during their visit. Use your self-awareness to conduct yourself in a professional and friendly manner.

Most agents like to scout the house on their own, but it is essential that you are well prepared to answer any of their questions. A good strategy is for you to sit down with your client and anticipate any questions—tax information or utility bills, for example—that you think agents might ask about. It is also good policy to anticipate any criticisms/objections that clients might offer—the price is too high; it needs a lot of work—and arm yourself with effective responses. Doing so will take some of the sting out of their criticisms, and because you are prepared, you will come across as knowledgeable, not defensive. It is also smart to have information that you know will be asked printed out—annual taxes, utility bills, square footage, and distance from schools—as this is information they will want to present to their clients. The less information you are asked for, the better your chances to stimulate interest.

Another way to apply emotional intelligence during a showing is to create positive affect—good feelings, favorable moods. There is a considerable amount of social psychology research that indicates that when individuals are feeling good, they make much more favorable judgments, and overlook negatives, be it of a person or an event. Thus, your strategy is to create positive affect in the visiting agents.

One way you can implement this cunning ploy is to have a table of goodies—not too healthy. Studies have shown that cookies are a good mood inducer, so it makes sense to have a box or three scattered throughout the house you are showing. A second way to create positive feelings is music. If the house has a stereo system, utilize it by playing some nice background music, not too loud, but at a level that is influential. These two positive mood inducers can tip the scales in your favor by getting the visiting agents to feel good about what they are seeing, and thus, give a favorable account to their clients.

If an agent or two makes a sarcastic comment about the house and raises an objection, use your self-awareness to help manage your emotions, and interpersonal expertise to respond non-defensively. If you have taken the earlier suggestion of anticipating and preparing for these comments, you will do fine, and remember to communicate on a factual level of information exchange. Thank each agent for coming. Let them know you are aware they are busy and appreciate them taking the time out to visit. Be sure to tell them that if they think of any questions, or if their clients have any questions they cannot answer, to just give you a call.

You might also find an opportunity to use the "Listerine technique." Nobody needs to tell you that Listerine tastes terrible; you know as soon as you use it. Studies show that when you make a negative comment about your product, the very next comment has enhanced credibility. Thus, if an agent is going to see something that is clearly negative, or find out a negative on his or her own, it makes sense to point it out and then immediately offer a positive. The positive you state is believed because you have demonstrated that you are "honest" by pointing out the negative. The beauty of course, is that by stating the negative, you are not telling the agent anything that he or she wouldn't find out anyway.

Here is an example. An EI real estate agent was showing a waterfront house. It was obvious that the side driveway would flood during heavy rainstorms and create a nuisance to the homeowner for a few days. Potential buyers would use this point to negotiate a lower price. So, this particular EI real estate agent said, "When there is a heavy rain and the river overflows, the driveway gets flooded, but after a day or two, the water flows back into the river, and you are left with a beautiful property, and the flooding only happens a few times a year. The second half of the statement is what sticks in the agent's mind.

Showing a house to a bunch of agents can be a nerve-racking and disastrous experience, but if you apply your EI, you can get great results, and for your client, you can "show them the money!"

5A. Meeting With Clients About Making an Offer

GOAL: To get the client to make a concrete, realistic offer
EI COMPETENCY: Emotional mentoring
SKILLS: Dealing with the client's emotions; achieving the
                   client's realistic expectations

You work with clients in two ways: You help them sell their house, and you help them buy their home. First, let's deal with representing the buying client.

Assuming you've found your clients their dream house, your task is to get them to make a concrete, realistic offer, defined as one the seller will likely accept.

Many times, a first-time buyer will make a concrete offer that is so off that there is no chance the seller will accept, and might even be offended by the offer to the point that they actually tune out future bids by the same buyer. This typically happens when the buyer is not emotionally ready to purchase a home, but wants to get his or her feet wet by going through the process, similar to the person who looks at a new car, but really is not ready to buy it. Of course, many times these buyers go on to make a purchase, but that is often months later.

Thus, start by assessing their *realistic commitment*. Do they really want this house? Of course, they will say yes, but you need to help them become aware of what that means. Say, "On a scale of one to ten, with ten meaning you must have it, assign a number to your buying commitment." In today's volatile economy, anything under a nine tells you and them that they are not as serious as they think, and that perhaps this isn't the right house. In other words, your clients need to have a very high buying commitment to the home; otherwise you might be wasting your time.

Remember that you can regulate their buying commitment by varying the listing price. The best and quickest way to do this is to simply ask, "At what price, without further negotiation, would you definitely buy the house?" Regardless of the answer, follow up with, "What is the very most you would pay for this house?" Again, regardless of the answer, "So if it were a thousand more, you wouldn't want it." Your strategy is to ask a series of questions designed to help the buyer become aware of what is the most he will offer to buy the particular house. If you have built a trusting relationship, he will disclose this information.

Based on the buyer's response and the data you have collected, you will know if there is a realistic chance for a successful purchase. If not, you can let the buyer go through the motions, but suggest a better strategy to look for a home that is within his price range, and that he will like more.

Let's say the buyer's offering price is realistic, but he or she is still hesitant to put it in writing. Such a circumstance tells the emotionally intelligent real estate agent that the client is experiencing anxiety. Remember, anxiety communicates uncertainty, so your task is to figure out what the client is uncertain about. Is it a financial issue? Perhaps it is whether or not their marriage is going to last, or maybe it has to do with whether or not they want to stay in the area for more than a few years. Whatever it is, it is preventing them from making their offer. The best way to handle the situation is to make their anxiety surface so that it can be confronted. Do this by being direct. Ask, "What exactly are you uncertain about that is preventing you from making an offer?"

If there is a hesitancy to respond, offer suggestions, such as, "Maybe you don't think you can really afford it. Let's go over the finances so that you can see that you can." "Perhaps you think there is a better house for you. We've looked for months, and this seems to be the best, but if you'd like, we can keep on looking." In both cases, it will be beneficial to use hard data. "Your income and tax returns show you can easily handle the payments." "We've looked at twenty houses over the last six months, and this is the one you like the best." Hardcore data is concrete and thus an antidote to feelings of uncertainty because it offers objectivity and shows that the "subjective feelings" of anxiety are actually unfounded.

If it is more of a personal nature, you might say, "It is probably best for you and your partner to have further discussion on whether or not you really want to make this commitment. Let me know what you decide."

You can alleviate the client's anxiety by saying, "Remember, you don't have to buy this home. I want you to feel good about making the commitment." Paradoxically, you will find that giving the client permission to walk away will increase the feeling that the buyer is in "control," and this tends to reduce anxiety and increase feelings that he or she is ready to commit.

Add to the commitment momentum by using positive expectations with statements like, "I know you are going to be happy." "This is such a great house/deal for you."

If still a bit of hesitancy remains, you may have to create some pressure to decide. This is accomplished by leveraging time. You might say, "You don't have to make an offer, but there is a great chance that someone else will make an offer in the next few days. It is a hot property, and it will go fast."

Remember, there is nothing unethical about using pressure to help a client make a decision—in this case, an offer that is in the buyer's best interest. Actually, you are doing him or her a favor.

5B. Meeting With the Client About Getting an Offer

GOAL: To get the client to appraise the offer and accept or make a counteroffer

EI COMPETENCY: Emotional mentoring; interpersonal expertise

SKILLS: Managing the client's emotions; realistic expectations, negotiation, listening

Now, you're on the other side of the table. You are presenting an offer to Mr. and Mrs. Jones. It is no problem if the offer matches their asking price, or is a bit lower but still acceptable and doesn't merit further negotiation. If this is the case, final paperwork is the next step.

However, more often than not, you will be presenting a number that does not match their asking price and is typically below their expectation. This is the time you need to apply your emotional intelligence in the form of emotional mentoring, and interpersonal expertise.

Any time you are going to present an offer that you know is below your client's expectations, it is good policy to anticipate their emotional response. You do this for two reasons.

The first is to prevent you, via emotional contagion, from catching the client's emotion, which will typically be anger—"Are they nuts? No way we are selling for that price!" or, dejection—"That's all? Gosh, it is much worse than I thought. We are in trouble." If you catch your clients' emotions, there is little chance that you will be able to help them. An angry real estate agent does not help an angry client—it makes the situation much worse. A dejected real estate client is not uplifting to a dejected and disappointed client—you might as well take the house off the market.

When you anticipate the client's emotions, you can immunize yourself to catching them. In the case of anger and anxiety, you can use your *relaxation response* and your *emotional management statements*. You might say to yourself, "Stay calm; I will help the client by being cool, focused, and relaxed." If you anticipate the client to be dejected or disappointed, use your self-motivation to "keep yourself up," so that you are enthusiastic, which will keep you from catching the "gloom and doom" scenario your client is likely to paint.

Most importantly, anticipating your clients' emotions is a reminder that their emotional landscape is their responsibility, not yours. Just because your client is angry or dejected does not mean you have to feel the same. Similarly, if your partner is depressed or angry, you need not feel the same. If you do, you cannot help them.

The second reason for anticipating your clients' emotions is that it affords you the opportunity to develop a strategy for effectively dealing with them.

Recall that emotions communicate information, and your strategy will be based upon the message of the emotion. Anger communicates that something is wrong; in this case, what is wrong, in the client's mind, is an unfair price. Determine whether this is true or not by using data, such as comparative sales, current market conditions, mortgage rates, how long the house has been on the market, and other information that your technical expertise uses in determining fair value. If you objectively decide it is an unfair offer, steer the client in making a realistic counteroffer, and follow traditional good faith negotiations.

However, more often than not, the offer is fair, but since it is below the client's expectations, it creates anger. Your goal now is to *help the client achieve realistic expectations* so that he or she can see that the offer as realistic and perhaps an excellent selling opportunity.

After you have *validated* the client's anger, you can best achieve your goal by *objectifying* the offer. Do this by presenting the data that you used to determine the fact that it is a fair offer. The more you mention the data, the quicker you will bring the client's anger under control, as the client will start to see that no matter how angry he or she is, it is not going to change the value of the house.

You can buffer the client's anger with the statement, "Well, if you don't want to sell or make a counteroffer, you don't have to. You can wait for another offer, but based on everything we have reviewed, I doubt it will be better, and who knows when or if it will come." The last segment of this sentence creates client anxiety (uncertainty), and in this context, the uncertainty of not getting a better offer will serve as a motivator to at least make a counteroffer. Using the same logic, you can say, "If you want, you can wait for market conditions to change, but that will probably take another six months to a year, and the market might even get worse."

If the anger persists, take advantage of the fact that when anger arousal decreases, angry thinking dissipates, leaving the individual a clearer mind to assess the situation. For example, let's say you are angry about a particular event on a Monday, but by Wednesday, the same event is non-anger provoking. The event has stayed the same, but your interpretation is different. Implement this point by saying, "Take a few days to think about it. If you still think it is unfair, we can reject it, or we can make a counteroffer that we think is appropriate." Note the phrase, "We can." This implies that you and the client are a team and will promote a sense of cooperativeness rather than the client blame you for the offer, as blame is typically a pal of angry feelings.

You can also lessen the anger by using *time pressure*: "I know you are disappointed with the offer, but the client's agent told me this is their best offer, and if we don't accept in two days, they will withdraw and go for another home. It is your decision." Using this technique, do not fall into the trap that you are unethically manipulating the client. You have already assessed that it is a fair offer and fully believe it is in the client's best interest to take the price. Of course, the time pressure condition is true, not something you are fabricating.

Ultimately, you help the angry client move through his anger by getting him to think, "What is the best action to take?" The answer is clearly not to remain angry, but to either to take the offer or make a counteroffer. With either response, you can move on to negotiation, or simply hope for another offer from another client.

What if the client is dejected? Like with angry client, validate the feelings. Say, "It is disappointing when you don't get what you were hoping for, and/or someone else doesn't see the same value in the home you love. Nevertheless, as your agent, I do think it is an offer for you to consider, or at least make a counteroffer."

When an individual is disappointed, there is usually a temporary loss of energy. As with the client who responds with anger, use your data to help restore the client's perception that the offer is fair and that his or her initial expectation was unrealistically high. This usually takes time, so you might say, "Take a few days to think about it, and I think you will realize that, considering market conditions, it is a realistic offer." Note, you did not say "good offer," because it isn't—but it is a *realistic* offer.

It is also smart to refurbish the trust your client has in you. It is easy for the client to transfer the disappointing offer into a feeling that you have let him down, and thus, lose confidence in your ability to get him the listing price. To restore trust, try saying, "Hey, I know you are disappointed, but remember, my job is to get you the best offer. In these times, my technical expertise tells me that this is the best offer we can expect. I wouldn't tell you to seriously consider it unless I really believed it. In fact, I have discussed this with other agents, and they agree, so you can feel comfortable in trusting my judgment. Think about it."

If the disappointment is evoked by an offer that is truly below fair market value, or if there are no offers at all, use emotional contagion to work for you. Use your self-motivation to make yourself enthusiastic. Maybe listen to some upbeat music before you meet with the client to discuss the situation.

When you meet, point out that according to data, the listing price is accurate, and you are confident that you will get a fair price, although it might take time. Assure the client that there is no need to panic, and if he or she desires, there is the option of taking the offer, although the seller can always get a similar offer in the future. Let the client know this is the worst scenario, implying that it can only get better. Your words, mixed with your body posture and enthusiasm, will help the client catch your positive outlook and feel optimistic about getting an offer in accordance with realistic expectations.

A third reaction to bringing a client a realistic offering is anxiety. Here, the client shows a general hesitancy to accept the offer. "I don't know if I should accept it" is the attitude, and the behavior is to procrastinate the decision, and say, "Hmm, maybe we'll get another offer."

In this scenario, the anxiety has little to do with the offer, especially since it is fair value—if not, the client would be angry or disappointed. Rather, the anxiety can be traced to a deeper uncertainty of whether or not the client is really committed to sell. Those who have lived in their homes for a long time, who are recently widowed or divorced, with no financial pressure, or who are empty nesters, are frequently anxious sellers. Use your emotional intelligence to flush out and probe their feelings. Specifically, are they ready to move on with their life?

It makes no sense to ask what price they would definitely accept because their answer will be totally unrealistic. It is equally ineffective to present data, because the offering price is not the reason for their anxiety; if it were, they would make a realistic counteroffer instead of procrastinating the decision.

Rather, you will be effective by gently offering, "Folks, it is a solid offer, and if you don't accept it or make a counteroffer, well, maybe you are really not ready to move. I think you really need to think through whether or not you want to sell your house, and if you don't, let's just take it off the market until you feel you are ready. On the other hand, if you feel you're ready to sell, then I think you have a very good offer in front of you. Think about it, and let your feelings guide you—they will help you make the right decision." Whatever they decide, you support them.

Note that in this case you would not use time pressure because the offer per se is not the issue—personal feelings are. Thus, you would be forcing the client to take an action that later they would regret, not for financial reasons, but for personal reasons, and this is never the intention of the emotionally intelligent real estate agent.

Once you have an acceptable offer, your commission is within reach. You just need to close the deal.

6. Closing the Deal

GOAL: Complete the negotiation
EI COMPETENCIES: Interpersonal expertise; mood management, self-motivation
SKILLS: Maintaining trust, shutting down anxiety, creating enthusiasm, following through

You have an enthusiastic buyer, an acceptable offer, and a happy client. What could go wrong? Plenty. Finance falls through, a disturbing house inspection, a low appraisal, and a failure to complete agreed upon repairs are all factors that can cause a last-minute stumble. Your job is to make sure they don't, so you can cross the goal line. Remember, it is not a deal until the check clears.

Closing the deal will become easier when you apply your self-awareness, keep emotions in check, and self-motivate to take care of all essential tasks that lead to check clearing.

Start with your real estate self-awareness. You are not going to re-member or be aware of all the factors that could cause you to stumble, so apply your self-motivation with a time lock and focal lock to make a list of all the factors that need to be taken care of, and—very impor-tant—anything you can imagine that could cause last-minute havoc. The first part of your list is your "tasks to complete." The second part of the list is to help you develop strategies of what to do if particular problems arise. The advantage of this self-assignment is that it will allow you to stay on course and, like a naval officer, respond with rapid deployment in case of a crisis. The faster you respond, the more likely you'll prevent a deal from breaking apart.

Many real estate agents experience anxiety while closing a deal. Here is where managing your emotions comes into play. Remember that anxiety communicates uncertainty, so instead of letting your anxiety make you forgetful and keep you from sleeping, use it as a cue to identify what you are uncertain about. Perhaps it's whether the appraisal will be acceptable to the bank, or whether the house inspection will be satisfactory, or whether you will get the recognition you think you deserve for making this deal. Once you know what you are uncertain about, you can attend to it appropriately.

As to your clients' anxiety, your best move is to keep them informed by supplying them with constant updates of the deal status. If they have tasks to complete, such as making a house repair, having a dumpster removed from the grounds by a specific date, gently urge them to take care of these "assignments," and remind them failing to do so could delay their goal. This is a good example of how you can use the client's anxiety to motivate them to take care of business. Be supportive and help them when you can. You might tell them that you'll call the Dumpster people for them and schedule the removal. This is a means to prevent them from dropping the ball.

More than ever, your interpersonal expertise needs to be applied by having frequent and open communication with the other agent involved in the deal. Be professional—not pushy—and have conversations with the goal being to assess whether his or her client is on the closing track. One useful strategy is to arrange structured "check-in conversations," a specific time where you will talk to review progress and what needs to be done. This is a far cry from the typical agents who say, "We will talk later (or soon)." Having a specific check-in conversation time increases responsibility to each other and keeps both of you fully engaged in the closing process.

If a problem arises, your anticipated problem list might provide the solution. If it doesn't, remember the key is to respond effectively, not with anger, anxiety, or fear. Rather, consider, "What is the best action to take?" Brainstorm with the other parties to come up with the answer, and you are sure to come up with a win-win action.

Of course, there are times that, regardless of what you do, the deal will fall apart. It might be that the client cannot attain the necessary financing. If you are the buyer, it might be that a housing inspection reveals such problems that your client decides to walk away. These problems are part of the business, and although they do occur, more often than not, they don't.

Plus, if you have done your homework in the listing stage and meet with the clients in making or accepting an offer, many of these deal breakers can be detected and prevented, and if not, at least save all parties the time of moving unproductively forward.

Maintain a positive attitude and enthusiasm by continually reminding your client and the other agent that the deal is almost complete. With your own client, continually reiterate how great her move/next chapter is going to be, and this will accentuate her enthusiasm, supplying her with energy to take care of her deal responsibilities.

To keep yourself motivated, confident, optimistic, and tenacious, be sure to use your check list as a reminder that you are approaching the goal line. Keep it in a high visibility location—your desk, taped to your computer, maybe on your home fridge. Every time you look at it, you will be reminded of what needs to be done as well as the progress you are making. Together, these thoughts help you move forward.

Inevitably, you cross the goal line, deal closed, check cashed! Congratulations.

FOUR

Your EI Real Estate Agent
APPS

OVER THE LAST FEW YEARS, I've had the pleasure of speaking at many real estate companies, conferences, conventions, and to dozens of agents and managers who have attended executive education classes. While the content of presentations often changes, all real estate agents seem to have some core issues and questions that represent their daily challenges. Based on my experiences and my hard listening, here are the most frequent questions, and, at least according to follow-up procedures, proven effective responses:

1. How do you deal with the ups and downs of the market?

First, make your expectations realistic by recognizing that "ups and downs" are not unique to real estate but are part of any industry. Failure to acknowledge this fact will always cause you frustration, anger, and sometimes depression. In short, you'll become a thermometer—when the market is good, you'll feel fine, and when it is down, you'll become distressed. This is a terrible way to live because you become a slave to the conditions of your environment. Transform yourself into a thermostat, so that regardless of market conditions, you can still feel good. Do this with a potpourri of mood management principles starting with awareness of your self-statements.

Remember that it is not the event that causes your emotional reaction, but rather *your interpretation of the event* that impacts you, for better or for worse. If you are feeling down when the market's down, your thoughts are along the lines of, "This is terrible, and I will never make a living." Thoughts such as these go on to evoke feelings of frustration, dejection, and despair. The thermostat in the same down market, thinks, "Down markets are part of the game; it won't last forever; just keep focused." These thoughts evoke feelings of optimism, confidence, and tenacity—the attributes that are required to make it through down times. When things are bad, we tend to experience gloom and doom, so remember to utilize your humor skills.

Examine your thoughts for cognitive distortions:
Imperative thinking: I should be doing better.
Magnification: This is the worse time ever, a disaster.
Overgeneralization: No house is selling; everything is slow.

Cognitive distortions are popular in your thinking when the market is down, and they fuel your negative perception of the market, making you more distressed and reinforcing your general negative thinking style. Use your emotional distress as a cue that it is time to reexamine your thinking, and you will quickly be alerted to the fact that your thinking is not helping you but making you feel worse. Then, challenge the truth value of your distortions, and you will begin to feel better.

Take a humor break each day. Find a few minutes to read your favorite joke book, or reminisce about something that will tickle your funny bone. So that you're not thrown off course, use time lock and focal lock to keep you focused on productive actions. Also, don't forget to use your support system to encourage and motivate you when your self-motivation weakens.

Together, these EI apps will help you deal effectively with the inevitable ups and downs of the real estate market.

2. How do you deal with couples who don't agree with each other?

This is a frequent occurrence when couples are getting divorced. One party wants to sell ASAP, and the other wants to maximize the profit. These agendas are frequently conflicting.

If you encounter this situation and the couple is not getting divorced, it is pretty valid to assume that the couple does not have the most harmonious relationship, perhaps because one of the partners actually does not want to sell their home. Remember that you are a real estate mediator, not a marriage mediator, so your first action is to make sure both parties are at least in agreement to sell. You might say, "Folks, maybe you need to take a week or two to really decide if both of you want to sell your house. This is something you need to figure out together. If you do, call me. If not, let me know if you ever want to sell, and I will help you."

Let's say they do want to sell. Your task is to increase each partner's awareness to what is a realistic listing price in the context of their time frame for selling, their financial situation, and all the other factors that your technical expertise tells you are important. Your apps are listening skills, levels of communication, and negotiation.

When the couple has discrepant ideas of what their house should be listed for, emotions can get out of hand, so you need to keep emotions in check. Do this by communicating on a factual level.

Not to play favorites, show both partners that you respect their views by asking them to present their facts. Say, "A good place to start is for each of you to tell me how you arrived at your listing price. Also, for me to help you, I need you to agree that after we look at all the data, if you don't agree, I will have the deciding vote. If not, I am not sure if I can help you, because it has to be a price that I believe is valid."

One party might say, "Well, this is what my friends say." If you hear that, respond with, "Well, are your friends real estate agents?" Or, you could say, "If you are going to listen to your friends, you certainly don't need me." Remember, in the case of discrepant listing prices, one of the parties, or maybe even both, is being unrealistic, so you need to keep the information exchange on a factual level. This serves two purposes: It keeps emotions in check, and sticking to the data rather than sub-jective opinions will minimize defensiveness in the unrealistic party, and help move one of them to the position of his or her partner. Make sure you summarize the rationale each partner presents, and then, be-ing the expert, present your views, the data it is based upon, and what you think the best price is in the context of the aforementioned factors.

What if one of the partners remains resistant, or if both do? "Well, I disagree with both of you, but it is your house. I certainly want to get you the best offer possible—that is to my advantage, too—so, how about we try your listing price for a specific amount of time? If we get a buyer, great; if we don't, we drop the price to a number that is agreed upon. Also, since I am being upfront with you that I disagree with your position, if the house doesn't sell, please don't do what many sellers do, which is to blame the agent. I only take responsibility for speed of sale when it is the listing price I recommend." The end point will be sure to come in handy when, most likely, the house doesn't sell.

3. How do you deal with unrealistic clients?

Unrealistic clients are burdensome to real estate agents because their unrealistic expectations waste a lot of time and detract from the main goal of selling or buying a house at the best price, in the short-est amount of time. Your apps will be managing your emotions, emo-tional mentoring of the client, and formulating realistic expectations.

Dealing with a client who has unrealistic expectations—or with anyone who does—is apt to create feelings of frustration because the client is preventing you from meeting your goal, which is to sell the house. Keep your frustration at a minimum by practicing your humor skills, using your relaxation response when dealing with the client, reminding yourself that unrealistic clients are the norm, and developing a strategy to get the client to become realistic in his or her expectations.

Get the client to articulate how he arrived at his expectation, whether it is a time frame for selling, a listing price, or a buying price. Then, in an educational—not argumentative—style, provide the facts that will bring his expectations to reality.

You can also try letting the client test his expectation. You might say, "Okay, let's make this offer and see what the client says. Maybe I am wrong." At the very worst, you get a counteroffer that will move the client into more realistic grounds. This is the same strategy to use if you are trying to sell his home at an unrealistic price.

If expectations remain unrealistic, you might try humorous exaggeration. Try, "Why not list it for two million instead of just a million (when it should be listed for eight hundred fifty thousand)?" Such a tactic often tells the clueless client that if he or she is going to over list (or underpay), it might as well be done in style. The typical response will be, "Don't be ridiculous," to which you should reply, "Well, in all due respect, your expectation, based on market conditions, is ridiculous."

If the client still refuses to budge, say, "Listen, I can't help you if you honestly think you are being realistic. I suggest you rethink your position, and when you are ready to be more realistic in your listing price or the quality of house you can buy in your price range, let me know, and I would love to help you." If the client calls you a week or two later, you have a realistic client; if not, you've gotten rid of your frustration!

4. How do you stay focused when you deal with many clients?

All of your clients want your focus, and if you have many of them, you are probably feeling stressed out, unless you know how to manage the demands they make, and focus effectively. Fortunately, there are several apps to help you.

If you are mishandling your stress, you can't be of help to anyone, so it is imperative you use your relaxation response daily. This will prevent sudden outbursts of frustration and anger, which do not serve your best interest or the best interest of your clients. Practice your humor skills daily, too. The more at ease you are, the more effective you will be at responding to client demands.

Next, recognize that although you are in a people business, it is really the deal that needs to be attended to, not the person. You can spend hours dealing with your favorite client, but if there is no action on his or her house deal, you are actually wasting valuable time. Deals—each associated with a particular client—need to be your priority, not the client, and by attending to the deal, you are, in effect, responding to the client.

Create a deal/client scorecard, the purpose of which is to help you keep score on where you are with each deal/client in the real estate process, the date of last contact, when you need to have your next contact, and whether it is a phone call, e-mail, or face-to-face meeting, and what needs to be done to further the deal. The purpose of the client scorecard is to help you prioritize the deals and prevent specific clients from falling through the cracks. A deal that can close in a week, if financing is approved, has more priority than a deal in which the client is just beginning cosmetic fix-up.

Time lock each day with the focal lock being to review your scorecard, which will tell you what deal you need to attend to that day. Then, proceed to contact those clients with the intent to progress the deal. You will find that the higher the deal priority, the more you will be focusing on deal logistics; the lower the priority, the more you will focus on relationship factors, like keeping the client optimistic and encouraging him or her to follow through on his or her responsibilities. Because you will be responding to the deal, the client will feel as though you are focused on his or her needs, and when you contact those for relationship reasons, the client will feel as though you are focused on him or her as a person.

If a client tells you that you are not focused on his or her needs, simply ask, "Well, where are you in the process? Have you taken care of the cosmetic repairs? Have you applied for a loan? There is nothing to do until you take care of these responsibilities. If you want me to help you, let me know."

Remember, you will be ineffective if you adapt a random strategy of trying to attend to all your clients. Keeping a client scorecard will help you stay focused when the heat is on.

5. What is the best way to deal with the strain that long hours put on family relationships?

You might be selling more houses than any other agent, but if you can't buffer the stress that the life puts on your family relationships, you might end your day in an empty home.

Balancing the needs of your clients and other demands of your job with the needs of your family and marriage are challenging tasks for any real estate agent, especially when today's market is more stressful than ever.

You need your family's support, so start by communicating realistic expectations about the nature of your work. You might try, "Listen, work is tough, and it is going to require that I spend a lot of time with clients, seeing houses and making phone calls. It is going to prevent me from spending a lot of time at home, and I can only be successful if I feel confident that you are all behind me. It is tough on me to be away from home so much, and I know it is tough on you. I need your support." Most likely you will get it. The problem that most agents make is that they are not truthful and upfront about the time they have to commit to work, so their families are constantly disappointed when duty calls. Let them know you are on twenty-four-hour call, and this will help them be realistic in their expectations.

The next app to use is a personal time lock in which you are unavailable to clients and other work-related issues. Don't fall into the trap that a deal is going to collapse because you don't respond rapidly or that a client is going to take a listing away from you. It does happen, but very, very rarely. During your personal time lock, your focal lock is time with your family. It might include dinner, watching television together, going for a walk—whatever the family and your partner enjoys. Do a personal time lock at least twice a week. It will be a stress reducer, and the good feelings it creates for everyone will energize family relationships.

Periodically, do a surprise special family event—you have to come up with this one on your own. Your thoughtful surprise will remind your family how much you love them.

Most importantly, be self-aware of the importance of your family and your partner. Doing so will make it easier for you to act out on your intentions of valuing them, namely, by spending quality time with them. Remember, a happy family makes a happy home-seller.

6. How do you deal with office politics and competitiveness?

Office politics and competitiveness go together like a horse and carriage, but do not make a happy marriage or a happy real estate agent. You don't need either.

Your apps to rid yourself of these interrelated plagues are cooperation and likeability builders, both of which are easy to use.

Competition, like politics, is a zero-sum game—somebody wins, somebody loses, and my experience tells me nobody likes to lose, and it is too much pressure to always have to win. Thus, in all your office encounters—office meetings and meetings with other agents you are working with—emphasize common goals; they get everybody going in the same direction. You might say, "Let's remember our goal of being the top branch in the company." "We can both win big on this transaction." Use cooperative words, like *we* and *our*, instead of *I, me,* or *you,* which often imply a sense of individual ownership, an impetus that fosters competitiveness.

Cooperation, like your life, is a give-and-take, so practice strategic reciprocity. Do this by performing favors for others—your assistant, office manager, other agents, and clients. Evolutionary scientists tell us that we are all hardwired for reciprocity, so doing favors for others triggers their cooperative instinct to respond in turn. In short, you can obligate people to be cooperative by doing favors for them. A favor for the secretary is likely to increase the chances that she will be sure to give you your messages instead of being forgetful, or to tell you first about the couple who walked into the office cold-calling for a real estate agent. After a while, because cooperation creates positive benefits, the relationship becomes a cooperative entity. Practice strategic reciprocity with all.

Point out that the office, like the human body, works best when there is a division of labor. Your legs might not like doing the walking after your stomach digests the good meal, but if both do their job, the body lives longer. While you have your own practice, you still are interdependent on others—agents to show you their listings, office staff to facilitate paper work, manager to give you leads—so maximize this point to show how it is in everyone's best interest to know they can rely on each other.

You can also turn competitiveness into cooperation by building an office with a positive, winning identity. It might sound hokey, but people do like to be part of a winning team. A team name, caps to wear in the office, T-shirts with the office logo, and nicknames for everyone, are all means to a cooperative end.

Be likeable—it makes others want to cooperate with you. Achieve this goal by praising, listening, and encouraging those you need to be supportive to you. You will see results quickly.

Perhaps the best way to handle office politics is to not engage in them. Stay focused, do your job, and cooperate with others.

7. How do you stay motivated when working independently?

It can be lonely at the top, but you will never get there if you can't work independently in a profession that basically demands you make your own way. Finding listings, getting buyers, dealing with financial institutions and lawyers, and doing mounds of paperwork are typically tasks that you do on your own, and are daunting, to say the least. It is a good thing there are apps to help you stay motivated.

Start each week by creating short-term goals. Do this by identifying your productive intentions—call specific clients, scout out new mortgages, look for new listings, are examples. Then time lock and focal lock each day to do the required behaviors that you need to do to realize these intentions. At the end of the week, you will see that you accomplished a lot, and the resulting good feelings of meeting your short-term goals will make you feel confident and help you stay motivated for achieving success.

Give yourself little rewards for achieving your short-term goals—a nice lunch, or maybe just some "goof-off time." It is not the reward, but the symbolic significance that you achieved what you intended to do.

If you feel a motivational lull, positively reminisce about your past successes. The good feelings they arouse will serve as current motivational energy.

Self-monitor your success. Construct a graph that shows the progress you are making on a specific goal—for example, seeing listings or calling clients. The visual of seeing yourself progress will encourage you to continue your efforts.

When a blast of motivation is needed, turn to your iPod. Sound communicates emotion, so some upbeat tunes will surely get you to pump out productivity.

Don't forget your emotional mentor—real or fictional. Thoughts of an inspirational individual will give you an energy boost to continue on your path.

Most importantly, engage in this exercise: Periodically reflect on the value of being in charge of your own destiny, determining your own income, and for the most part, having a flexible work style. Then, briefly entertain the thought of having to do a boring job. You will be so happy you are doing what you want that you will have no problem working independently and staying motivated!

8. How do you keep everyone at the table in a long negotiation?

It takes at least two to negotiate successfully, so you have to keep your partner in the dance.

A long negotiation, like a long dance, is tiresome, and it is easy for one party to want to stop. Maybe a better partner in the form of a better house is the dance disruption tap on the shoulder, or maybe it is an inadvertent stepping on the toes of your partner. Whatever the reason, a long negotiation can easily lead to a broken deal. Here are some side step apps to help you in the long negotiation:

Keep frustration in check via positive expectations. Frustration— the blocking of a goal—is common in a long negotiation, and the longer the negotiation, the more apt one or those involved may think it is never going to end, and thus, slowly start to look for alternatives. Deal with feelings of frustration by validating the frustration of everyone involved, and then keep it in check by noting the progress made, and state positive expectations, like "Hey, we are all feeling a little stymied, but this is going to happen; we are making great progress." The reminder of the progress made and the positive expectation that the deal will be successful is likely to keep the dance going until the song is complete.

Emphasize the common goal. A long negotiation is often caused by specific differences, which inevitably drive people apart. To keep it a close dance, emphasize the common goal. You might say, "We both agree on wanting to complete the deal." A common goal directs everyone in the same direction. Don't make the mistake of emphasizing differences, which cause people to separate. When disagreements surface, get back to emphasizing the common goal. Address them with, "Well, we all want to complete the deal, so let's figure out how to iron out the differences."

Remind each person that he or she wants the deal. In individual encounters, keep each person tuned to the fact. Try saying, "Listen, you want the house (or, you want to sell the house), so let's just work things out with the seller (or buyer), so you can get what you want."

Remember, in a negotiation, there has to be something in it for everybody, so point out the individual payoff to each individual.

Be an effective problem solver. To end the dance, it is smart to think, "The problem is not a long negotiation, but rather, how we are responding to the negotiation." Say to the group, "Hey, what we are all doing is not working. Let's think how we respond differently to the last few details, so we can all get what we want. Let's have a brainstorming session. We are all a little frustrated because we want the deal to close. We've made a lot of progress—financing is done, housing inspection is good. All we need to do is figure out how to handle the last few details so we all walk away winners."

If you apply the aforementioned steps, you will be able to dance—I mean, negotiate—the night away!

9. How do you get through a dry spell?

A dry spell can be a real estate agent's nightmare, but if it turns into reality, it is much scarier. Don't panic, though, because you don't have to be a prince, princess, or good witch to break the spell—just use some EI apps.

Use your feelings of dry spell distress as a cue to re-examine your thoughts. Typical dry spell thoughts are: "This is a disaster; I will never sell another house; I won't be able to pay my bills." Granted, these thoughts are distorted and irrational, but the fact is, these are accurate descriptions of how most real estate agents talk to themselves when the going gets tough, and these self-inflicted punches make a dry spell seem dryer. Once you are aware of them, counter-punch these statements with ones that help you keep perspective so that you can keep yourself going the distance. Say, "I can handle this. I've had dry spells before. All agents, not just me, are finding things slow. The market, like in the past, will turn around. I am good at what I do." These counter-punch statements will prevent you from feeling the frustration, anxiety, and frequent despair that often are experienced in a dry spell.

Focus on productive activities, not results. Sitting at your desk with self-pity is of no help, so make sure you fill your dry spells with time locks and focal locks to do those activities that inevitably will help you. By the end of the day, you will feel productive and energized.

Network yourself. Interacting with others is better than being by yourself and will prevent you from dropping into a bad mood. Furthermore, your social contacts will often lead you to a listing or a buyer, both catalysts to ending a dry spell.

Don't take it personally. Dry spells are typically a function of market conditions, not your performance. Remember this, and inevitably you will become a rainmaker!

10. How do you get clients to spend money to make their house a better listing?

Sometimes you have to spend money to make money. Few people can argue with this point, so your first task is to use your interpersonal expertise to find out why your clients won't cough up the dough.

Rarely does the client have to spend huge amounts of money. If that is the case, list it as a "fixer-upper," case closed. Most likely, it will be several thousand dollars for cosmetics. Yet, you will still hear the typical responses: "I can't afford it," "It is not going to make a difference," or, "If the buyer really wants the house, he will pay for it," Regardless of the answer, you need to overcome the objections.

Your best response is to clearly state the incentive for the client. Tell them that the house has a greater chance of selling if it is fixed up (landscaping, painting, reducing clutter, deck cleaning). "The house shows better with these fix-ups and will sell quicker," is your most direct statement.

If client is still resistant, you can emphasize the negative future consequences of such behavior: "If you don't fix it up, it will take a longer time to sell." The client doesn't have to deal with the negative consequence—longer time to sell—if he or she dolls the house up. Throw in a comparative statement: "Other houses in the same price range look a lot more attractive."

For some clients, reframing the reason for the spending is effective. You might say, "Look, the money you spend is a wise investment. It increases the value of the house, and will get you a better return." If countered with, "Not true, you only get half your money back," snap back with, "Yes, but half back is better than not selling it at all."

You can also increase the seller's anxiety to motivate some spending by saying, "Okay, don't do the fix-ups, but I doubt we will sell it. It is up to you."

For the more resistant, say, "Okay, we won't fix it up, we will just figure out how much these things would cost and lower the price accordingly, fair enough?"

If the response is still, "Let the client pay," you retort, "I'll try, but if he doesn't, then do you not want to sell it?"

Finally, you can counter with, "Well, if you don't make it look better, I can't be my most enthusiastic in representing it, because it just doesn't look good." Wait for a response, and if you deem worthy, say, "I will front the money, but when we sell it, I get the money back. I doubt you will get that offer from any other real estate agent!"

It is common practice among sellers to make their house look attractive before it goes on the market, so tradition is on your side. Sometimes you have to spend to make.

For all other difficult situations, think of and upload your own EI apps. You have plenty in you!

FIVE

Closing Points:
What the Emotionally
Intelligent Real Estate Agent
Always Remembers

ALL IT A SUMMARY if you want. To be an emotionally intelligent real estate agent (EIRA) for the long haul, there are four points with which you must always comply, and if you do, you will always be applying your emotional intelligence. The four closing points that emotionally intelligent real estate agents rigidly adhere to are:

1. *Awareness to intent:* The EIRA comes to work each day keenly aware that his intent is to be productive. As a result, he automatically begins using his thoughts as a motivating tool and to guide his behavior for achieving his results.

2. *Awareness to actions:* The EIRA is always paying attention to her actions so she can "keep an eye on herself," ensuring that her actions match her intent to be productive and, at the same time, ridding herself of behaviors that could block her success.

3. *Using emotions as cues for gauging the day:* The EIRA is adept at using his feelings—anger, stress, anxiety, enthusiasm—as a cue to how he is experiencing his day. If it's emotional distress, he knows it is time to examine his self-talk for negative messages, take a breather to regroup, realize he must generate a more effective response, or remind himself that an important issue is affecting him and must be confronted. If he is enthusiastic and feeling productive, he reminds himself of what he is doing and thinking that is making him feel great.

4. *Staying proactive:* The EIRA recognizes that success requires pro-activity. This belief becomes his or her impetus for self-motivation, turning setbacks into comebacks, problem solving, and going after new business opportunities.

When you are in compliance with these four points—congratulations! You are an Emotionally Intelligent Real Estate Agent!

Blueprint for Applying Your Emotional Intelligence

T HE BLUEPRINT for applying your emotional intelligence is a tool designed to help you integrate emotional intelligence into your daily functioning. The more you follow the blueprint, the more adept you will become at using your emotional intelligence. Doing it every day will yield results in a short time. For the blueprint to be effective, *all of the steps are mandatory and must be implemented as prescribed:*

EI PREPARATION BEFORE WORK

The following tasks are to be done *the night before* you go to work.

- *First thoughts:* On an index card, write down three statements that will help you start out the day on a positive note. Give the card high visibility on your night table and on your desk.

- *Practice relaxation for ten minutes:* When you practice relaxation, make sure that you conjure up a relaxing image and associate it with a key phrase.

- *Intentions for the day:* Write down three intentions that you have for the next day, such as calling certain clients, researching an investment, or setting up a presentation. Prioritize them with the first being the most important.

- *Behaviors:* Make a list of behaviors that you need to do to accomplish the intentions you have identified. Put them on an index card, take the index card to work, and put it on your desk so you can see it all day.

- *Time lock:* Identify several periods for doing the specific behaviors that will help you accomplish your intentions. Let people know you are time locking.

- *Focal lock:* Identify the necessary behaviors to do for each of your time locks.

- *Anticipate setbacks:* List three possible setbacks that you might encounter, such as a client leaving you, a canceled meeting with a hot prospect, a barrage of negative thinking, or interruptions to your time locks. Take a few minutes, and mentally rehearse how you would deal with each setback. Also, be aware of what emotional setbacks evoke in you and how you can manage these emotions.

- *Gather emotional information.* Make a list of emotions—anger, anxiety, fear, disappointment, enthusiasm—on an index card. Next to each, make a notation of how you will best manage that emotion when experiencing it. Put the card on your desk. Several times a day, ask yourself what emotions, at that moment, you are experiencing. Check your immediate thoughts, and examine your behavior to see if you are acting productively. If you are feeling anxious, for example, are you mentally paralyzed, or are you engaged in activities that help manage the anxiety? If the former, check your card.

- *Anticipate interpersonal encounters, phone calls, and meetings:* Make a list of each interpersonal encounter you are likely to have the next day, and write down your intentions for each anticipated encounter. Mentally rehearse how you will conduct yourself so that you make the encounter productive and achieve your desired results. Also, be sure to mentally rehearse how to conduct yourself and manage your emotions in interpersonal scenarios that are emotionally charged, such as your branch manager criticizing you at a staff meeting. Make sure you mentally rehearse effective responses for these situations.

APPLICATION AT WORK

- *Follow the blueprint.* Follow your blueprint exactly as you have planned it. Each day you follow it, it becomes easier to build your emotional intelligence.
- *Identify your successes.* At the end of the day, identify your successes, whether it is completing your time lock and focal lock, or giving an effective presentation. Reflect on these successes, and increase your awareness of how you conducted yourself to achieve your results. Be specific in your thoughts.

TROUBLESHOOTING:
IF YOUR BLUEPRINT ISN,,T WORKING

- It might be too hard for you to follow. Simply write down one intention instead of three; time lock once a day instead of twice.
- It may also be that you are not effectively implementing the content of each step. Perhaps your intentions are too general. Maybe you are not fully aware of the actions that are derailing you. Skill development and increasing your awareness will

help you construct and implement your blueprint, so reread the pages on these subjects.

Do the above every day for the next month. After that, you will have it imprinted into your emotional operating system.

References

Weisinger, Hendrie. 1995. *Anger at Work.* New York: William Morrow.

____. *Emotional Intelligence at Work.* 1998. San Francisco: Jossey Bass.

____. The *Power of Positive Criticism.* 2001. New York: AMACOM.

Hendrie Weisinger and L. Andrews, "Motivating Yourself When You're Stuck." Horsesmouth.com. September 25, 2001.

____. "Managing Your Emotions in Rocky Times." Horsesmouth.com. October 18, 2001.

____. "Staying Motivated for the Long Haul." Horsesmouth.com. January 17, 2002.

____. "5 Ways to Develop Self-Awareness." Horsesmouth.com. January 24, 2002.

____. "How a Skilled Communicator Talks and Listens." Horsesmouth. com. January 24, 2002.

____. "Fix Communication Breakdowns for Better Teams." Horsesmouth.com. February 7, 2002.

____. "Sharpen Interpersonal Skills to Reinforce Client Relationships." Horsesmouth.com. March 19, 2002.

____. "Reduce Stress and Stay Focused in Difficult Times." Horsesmouth.com. April 2, 2002.

____. "From Setback to Comeback In 7 Steps." Horsesmouth.com. May 20, 2002.

____. "Develop High Self-Awareness to Boost Productivity." Horsesmouth.com. May 28, 2002.

____. "When Every Work Counts: Talking with Clients." Horsesmouth. com. May 29, 2002.

____. "What Your 5 Senses Can Tell You about Clients." Horsesmouth. com. June 4, 2002.

____. "Taking Care of Your Behavior and Defusing Bad Habits." Horses-mouth.com. June 9, 2002.

____. "Good First Impression: Your Intentions Need to Match Your Actions." Horsesmouth.com. June 11, 2002.

____. "Speak Up and Get What You Want." Horsesmouth.com. September 17, 2002.

Index

About the Author

FEW PEOPLE have developed an expertise in areas that impact everybody, everyday, at home and at work, but that is exactly the case for creator, innovator, practitioner, world-renowned psychologist, and *New York Times* bestselling author, Dr. Hendrie Weisinger. Giving and taking criticism, managing emotions, responding effectively to the feelings and emotions of others, motivating oneself and others, and resolving conflict, are all "emotional intelligence skills" that are part of Dr. Weisinger's expertise and have been recognized and sought by leading business schools, influential government agencies, Fortune 500 companies, and dozens of professional organizations, such as The Young Presidents Organization.

Author of *Emotional Intelligence at Work, The Emotionally Intelligent Financial Agent, Dr. Weisinger's Anger Workout Book, Anger at Work, The Power of Positive Criticism*, and the New York Times bestseller, *Nobody's Perfect*, Dr. Weisinger has spent three decades helping individuals and their organizations enhance their personal and work effectiveness through innovative applications of clinical, social, organizational, and most recently, evolutionary psychology, with the publication of his latest book, *The Genius of Instinct*.

His early clinical training and practice provided him the opportunities to decipher the emotional complexities of giving and taking criticism back in the day when "feedback" was the choice word. His work in this area culminated in *Nobody's Perfect*. The success of this book put Dr. Weisinger in front of executives, managers, and supervisors, from corporate America. IBM, AT&T, Merck, Nintendo, Sheraton, Hughes Aircraft, General Electric, Medtronic, KMPG, McDonalds, The Hartford, Prudential, Hyatt, Estee Lauder, and Nabisco are just a small sample of companies that have requested Dr. Weisinger to present his message to their employees. The same is true for government agencies, such as the CIA, FBI, IRS, and NSA. Since *Nobody's Perfect*, Dr. Weisinger has continually advanced his theory and techniques for giving and taking criticism. His most recent thoughts captured in *The Power of Positive Criticism* translated into over a dozen languages. His article for *The Wall Street Journal*, "So You're Afraid to Criticize Your Boss?" was selected as one of the sixty best articles ever to appear in the Journal's Management Column and is reprinted in *Dow Jones on Management*. The article caught the eye of the executive education program at the UCLA Anderson Graduate School of Management, and since the 1980s, Dr. Weisinger has been a frequent lecturer in their executive education and executive MBA programs.

While his reputation in giving and taking criticism was growing in prominence, Dr. Weisinger was developing a second expertise and, like giving and taking criticism, one that is crucial to individual and organizational effectiveness: anger management. Long before it was a movie, Dr. Weisinger was integrating cognitive psychology, behaviorism, and interpersonal psychology to formulate the blueprint for the majority of anger management programs. He became one of the first psychologists to provide training in the subject to the mental health community, so it is not surprising that he has spoken to dozens of mental health organizations, hospitals, and school systems. His book

Dr. Weisinger's Anger Workout Book is a classic among mental health workers and is now in its twenty-eighth printing. No doubt this is one of the reasons that Dr. Weisinger appeared on *The Today Show* for five consecutive days during their anger management special, as well as on Oprah, and he was featured in *The New York Times* Sunday business section. As with giving and taking criticism, Dr. Weisinger applied his knowledge to the working world, the result being *Anger at Work*, and according to the Library of Congress, it is "highly recommended to managers at all levels."

In the mid '90s, Dr. Weisinger was thought to be a world expert in the area of emotional intelligence, a subject that he would lecture on at numerous business schools, including NYU, MIT, Penn State, the University of Washington, Cornell, and Wharton, where he is now one of their most popular and highly regarded executive education professors. His publications on emotional intelligence are numerous and diverse. His signature book on the subject, *Emotional Intelligence at Work*, is considered to be the best book on applying emotional intelligence and can be found on seven continents. Working with Merrill Lynch, Bank of America, Wachovia, Morgan Stanley Smith Barney, H&R Block, and numerous other financial service companies and making numerous presentations for the Security Industry Association, Dr. Weisinger became armed with the knowledge to write *The Emotionally Intelligent Financial Agent*, the first book on emotional intelligence to be customized to a specific industry. He is now doing the same for the nursing profession and project management profession. His article, "Tutored by Television" published in *TV Guide*, illustrates how parents can use television to develop the emotional intelligence of their children.

Always looking for innovative perspectives on human behavior, and always seeming to be ahead of the pack, Dr. Weisinger turned his interest to the evolutionary sciences, particularly evolutionary psychology. His studies in the field, now called "the new science of the mind," took him down a path that, when mixed with clinical expertise, provided startling new thoughts and strategies for handling every-day dilemmas that we all encounter at home and at work. His find-ings and observations are the subject of his most current work, *The Genius of Instinct: Reclaim Mother Nature's Tools for Enhancing our Health, Happiness, Family, and Work*. The book presents many revela-tions, including the fact that we are hardwired for success. Man is more successful than animals because we have more instincts, not less, and relying on reason rather than instinct typically spells disaster. This evolutionary perspective has also helped Dr. Weisinger generate novel insights into leadership, marriage, parenting, and work.

Contact Dr. Weisinger: drhankw.com.
Speaking Engagements: If you would like to have Dr. Weisinger speak to your organization, please call Mr. Derek Sweeney, 1-866-727-7555 or derek@thesweeneyagency.com.

www.ingramcontent.com/pod-product-compliance
Lightning Source LLC
Chambersburg PA
CBHW051214170526
45166CB00005B/1885